Charles Converse

Songs of the covenant

For the Sabbath-school, prayer-meetings, etc.

Charles Converse

Songs of the covenant
For the Sabbath-school, prayer-meetings, etc.

ISBN/EAN: 9783337265120

Printed in Europe, USA, Canada, Australia, Japan

Cover: Foto ©Lupo / pixelio.de

More available books at **www.hansebooks.com**

Songs of the Covenant

FOR THE

Sabbath-School, Prayer-Meetings, Etc.

C. C. CONVERSE,
EDITOR.

RICHMOND, VA.:
PRESBYTERIAN COMMITTEE OF PUBLICATION.
1892.

Copyrighted by Jas. K. Hazen, Sec. of Pres. Com. of Pub., 1892.
All rights reserved.

The pieces in this book marked "By per." are protected by this copyright and by the copyrights of their respective authors, and may not, therefore, be used in other books without the consent of their authors, even though the word "copyrighted" does not appear on them.

What a Friend We Have in Jesus.

C. C. CONVERSE. By per.*

1. What a friend we have in Je - sus, All our sins and griefs to bear;
2. Have we tri - als and temp-ta-tions? Is there trouble a - ny- where?
3. Are we weak and heavy la - den, Cumbered with a load of care?—

What a priv-i-lege to car - ry Ev-'ry-thing to God in prayer!
We should never be dis-cour-aged, Take it to the Lord in prayer!
Pre-cious Saviour, still our ref - uge,— Take it to the Lord in prayer!

O what peace we oft-en for - feit, O what needless pain we bear,
Can we find a friend so faith- ful, Who will all our sorrows share?
Do thy friends despise, forsake thee? Take it to the Lord in prayer;

All because we do not car - ry Ev - 'ry thing to God in prayer!
Je-sus knows our ev-'ry weakness, Take it to the Lord in prayer!
In His arms He'll take and shield thee, Thou wilt find a sol-ace there.

* All the pieces marked "By per." are protected from other than permitted use by their authors.

WE NEED A FRIEND LIKE JESUS.

5. Friend of Sinners.

Rev. NEWMAN HALL.   C. C. CONVERSE. By per.

1. Friend of sinners! Lord of glory! Lowly, Mighty! Brother, King! Musing o'er Thy wondrous story, Grateful we Thy praises sing: Friend to help us, cheer us, save us, In whom pow'r and pity blend — Praise we must the grace which gave us Jesus Christ, the sinners' Friend.

2 Friend who never fails nor grieves us,
  Faithful, tender, constant, kind! —
Friend who at all times receives us,
  Friend who came the lost to find! —
Sorrow soothing, joys enhancing,
  Loving until life shall end —
Then conferring bliss entrancing,
  Still, in heav'n, the sinners' Friend.

3 O to love and serve Thee better!
  From all evil set us free;
Break, Lord, every sinful fetter;
  Be each tho't conform'd to Thee:
Looking for Thy bright appearing,
  May our spirits upward tend;
Till no longer doubting, fearing,
  We behold the sinners' Friend!

3 Let sorrow do its work,
   Send grief and pain;
   Sweet are Thy messengers,
   Sweet their refrain,
   When they can sing with me,
   More love, O Christ! to Thee,
   More love to Thee!

4 Then shall my latest breath
   Whisper Thy praise;
   This be the parting cry
   My heart shall raise,
   This still its prayer shall be:
   More love, O Christ! to Thee,
   More love to Thee!

All for Jesus.

10. O Bread to Pilgrims Given.

Tr. by Rev. R. Palmer.   Arr. from Bellini.

1. O Bread, to pilgrims given,
O Food, that Angels eat,
O Manna sent from heav-en,
For heav'n-born natures meet!
Give us, for Thee, long pin-ing
To eat till rich-ly fill'd;
Till, earth's delights resigning,
Our ev'ry wish is still'd!

2 O Water, life bestowing,
  From out the Saviour's heart,
A fountain purely flowing,
  A fount of love Thou art!
Oh! let us, freely tasting,
  Our burning thirst assuage!
Thy sweetness, never wasting,
  Avails from age to age.

3 Jesus, this feast receiving,
  We Thee unseen adore;
Thy faithful word believing,
  We take, and doubt no more:
Give us, Thou true and loving,
  On earth to live in Thee;
Then, death the veil removing,
  Thy glorious face to see!

2 See, Jesus stands with open arms;
He calls, He bids you come;
Guilt holds you back, and fear alarms;
But see, there yet is room. Cho.

3 Room in the Saviour's bleeding heart:
There love and pity meet;
Nor will He bid the soul depart
That trembles at His feet. Cho.

4 There, with united heart and voice,
Before the heav'nly throne,
Ten thousand thousand souls rejoice
In ecstacies unknown. Cho.

12. Keep me near to Thee, dear Saviour.

J. A. GARDNER. C. C. CONVERSE. By per.

1. Keep me near to Thee, dear Saviour, ev-er keep me near to Thee, I am weak and prone to wander, Je-sus, keep me near to Thee! Keep me from all doubt and danger, keep me from all fear and blame. Keep me from all strife and anger, keep me from all sin and shame;

2. Keep me near to Thee, dear Saviour, ev-er keep me near to Thee, I am thine, and thine forev-er, Je-sus, keep me near to Thee! Keep me un-der Thy protection and the shadow of Thy wings: Keep from tri-al and cor-rec-tion, keep from lov-ing earthly things.

CHORUS.

Keep me near to Thee, dear Saviour, ever keep me near to Thee! Keep me near to Thee, dear Saviour, ev-er keep me near to Thee!

13. Soldiers of the Cross.

Arr. from Rossini. By per.

1. We are soldiers of the cross, Ours the old, old story;
Counting all our gains as loss, But the gain for glory.
In the path our fathers trod With their faith unswerving;
Heroes of the Church of God, So would we be serving.

2 As we raise our martial song,
   Courage ne'er abating;
Angel bands, a holy throng,
   On our steps are waiting.
Soon the journey will be o'er,
   Passed each dark affliction;
Let us think how Jesus bore
   Scourge and crucifixion.
      We are soldiers, etc.

3 See the heav'nly mansions bright
   Faithful hope adorning!
Far behind us looms the night,
   But before, the morning:
Onward, onward to the goal,
   Jesus goes before us;
Come, O come! each ransomed soul,
   Sound on high the chorus.
      We are soldiers, etc.

14. Sweetly Sing the Love of Jesus.

MARY VIRGINIA TERHUNE. Arr. from S. DE MEDEL. By per.

1. Sweetly sing the love of Jesus! Love for you, and love for me; Heaven's light is not more cheering, Heaven's dews are not more free. As a child in pain or terror, Hides him in his mother's breast, As a sailor seeks the haven, We would come to Him for rest.

2 Gladly sing the love of Jesus!
   Let us lean upon His arm.
  If He love us what can grieve us?
  If He keep us, what can harm?
  Still He lays His hands in blessing
   On each timid little face,
  And in heav'n the children's angels
   Near the throne have always place.

3 Ever sing the love of Jesus!
   Let the day be dark or clear,
  Every pain and every sorrow
   Bring His own to Him more near.
  Death's cold wave need not affright us
   When we know that He has died,
  When we see the face of Jesus
   Smiling on the Other Side!

15 Only remembered by what I have done.

Rev. H. Bonar.   C. C. Converse. By per.

1. Fading away, like the dew of the morning, Soaring from earth to its home in the sun;
Thus would I pass from the earth and its toiling, Only remembered by what I have done.

CHORUS.
Only remembered, only remembered, Only remembered by what I have done,
On-ly remembered, on-ly remembered, Only remembered by what I have done.

2 Shall I be missed if another succeed me,
   Reaping the fields I in spring-time have sown?
No, for the sower may pass from his labors,
   Only remembered by what he has done. Cho.

3 Oh! when the Saviour shall make up His jewels,
   When the bright crowns of rejoicing are won,
Then will His faithful and weary disciples
   All be remembered for what they have done. Cho.

16. The Sinner's Friend.

R. BURNHAM. MENDELSSOHN.

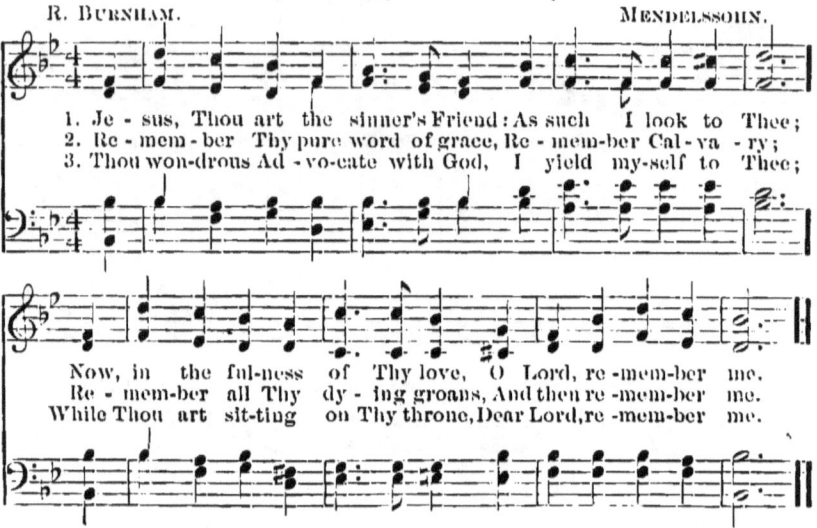

1. Je-sus, Thou art the sinner's Friend: As such I look to Thee;
   Now, in the ful-ness of Thy love, O Lord, re-mem-ber me.
2. Re-mem-ber Thy pure word of grace, Re-mem-ber Cal-va-ry;
   Re-mem-ber all Thy dy-ing groans, And then re-mem-ber me.
3. Thou won-drous Ad-vo-cate with God, I yield my-self to Thee;
   While Thou art sit-ting on Thy throne, Dear Lord, re-mem-ber me.

4 Lord, I am guilty, I am vile,
  But Thy salvation's free;
  Then in Thine all-abounding grace,
  Dear Lord, remember me.

5 And when I close my eyes in death,
  When creature-helps all flee,
  Then, O my dear Redeemer, God,
  I pray, remember me.

17. Everlasting Rest.

SIR R. GRANT. REV. R. P. KERR. By per.

1. Lord of earth, Thy forming hand Well this beaut'ous frame hath planned;
   Woods that wave and hills that tow'r, (Omit. . . . .) Ocean roll-ing in its pow'r;
   What were all its joys to me? (Omit. . . . .) Whom have I on earth but Thee?
   Yet a-mid this scene so fair, Should I cease Thy smile to share,
2. Lord of earth and heav'n, my breast Seeks in Thee its only rest;
   I was lost,—Thy accents mild (Omit. . . . .) Homeward lured Thy wand'ring child.
   What were earth or heav'n to me? (Omit. . . . .) Whom have I in each but Thee?
   Oh if once Thy smile di-vine, Ceased up-on my soul to shine.

Parting Song.

JOHN ELLERTON.   Arr. from DONIZETTI. By per.

1. Sav-iour, a-gain, to Thy dear Name we raise, With one ac-cord, our part-ing hymn of praise; We stand to bless Thee ere our worship cease, Then, low-ly bending, wait Thy word of peace.

2 Grant us Thy peace upon our homeward way;
With Thee began, with Thee shall end the day;
Guard Thou the lips from sin, the hearts from shame,
That in this house have called upon Thy name.

3 Grant us Thy peace, Lord, through the coming night,
Turn Thou for us its darkness into light;
From harm and danger keep Thy children free,
For dark and light are both alike to Thee.

4 Grant us Thy peace throughout our earthly life,
Our balm in sorrow, and our stay in strife;
Then, when Thy voice shall bid our conflict cease,
Call us, O Lord, to Thine eternal peace.

19. Heaven is My Home.

Adapted. By per.

1. { I'm but a stranger here, Heav'n is my home;
    Earth is a des-ert drear, Heav'n is my home; }
2. { What tho' the tem-pest rage? Heav'n is my home;
    Short is my pil-grim-age, Heav'n is my home; }

Dan-ger and sor-row stand Round me on ev-'ry hand;
Time's cold and win-try blast Soon will be o-ver-past;

Heav'n is my Fath-er-land, Heav'n is my home.
I shall reach home at last, Heav'n is my home.

4 There, at my Saviour's side,
  Heav'n is my home;
I shall be glorified;
  Heav'n is my home;
There are the good and blest,
Those I loved most and best,
There, too, I soon shall rest,
  Heav'n is my home.

20. Nearer My God, to Thee.

1 Nearer, my God, to Thee,
  Nearer to Thee!
E'en though it be a cross
  That raiseth me!
Still all my song shall be,
Nearer, my God, to Thee,
  Nearer to Thee!

2 Though like the wanderer,
  The sun gone down,
Darkness be over me,
  My rest a stone,
Yet in my dreams I'd be
Nearer, my God, to Thee,
  Nearer to Thee!

3 There let the way appear,
  Steps unto heav'n;
All that Thou sendest me,
  In mercy giv'n;
Angels to beckon me
Nearer, my God, to Thee,
  Nearer to Thee!

4 Then, with my waking thoughts
  Bright with Thy praise,
Out of my stony griefs
  Bethel I'll raise;
So by my woes to be
Nearer, my God, to Thee,
  Nearer to Thee!

5 Or, if on joyful wing
  Cleaving the sky,
Sun, moon and stars forgot,
  Upward I fly,
Still all my song shall be,
Nearer, my God, to Thee,
  Nearer to Thee!

Toiling Early.

C. C. Converse. By per.

1. Toiling early in the morning, Catching moments through the day, Nothing small or lowly scorning While we work, and watch, and pray; Gath'ring gladly, gath'ring gladly Free-will offerings by the way.

2 Not for selfish praise or glory,
   Nor for things of transient worth;
But to send the blessed story
   Of the gospel o'er the earth;
Telling mortals, telling mortals,
   Of our Lord and Saviour's birth.

3 Up and ever at our calling,
   Till in death our lips are dumb,
Or till — sin's dominion falling—
   Christ shall in His kingdom come;
And His children, ransomed children,
   Reach their everlasting home.

4 Steadfast then in our endeavor,
   Heav'nly Father, may we be;
And forever and forever,
   We will give the praise to Thee;
Alleluia, Alleluia,
   Singing all eternity.

22. While we Journey Homeward.

Arr. from FLOTOW. By per.

1. While we jour-ney homeward, let us Help each oth-er on the road; Foes on ev-'ry side be-set us, Snares thro' all the way are strew'd; It be-hoves us, it be-hoves us Each to bear a bro-ther's load.

D.C. Then let each es-teem his broth-er Bet-ter than him-self to be; And let each pre-fer an-oth-er, Full of love, from en-vy free.

2 When we think how much our Father
  Has forgiv'n and does forgive,
Brethren, we should learn the rather
  Free from wrath and strife to live,
    Far removing, far removing
  All that might offend or grieve. *D. C.* Then let, etc.

23. Jubilate Deo.

JOSEPHINE POLLARD.   KARL REDEN. By per.

1. Oh, be joyful all ye lands! Shout aloud for joy!
   Take your harps within your hands, Shout aloud for joy!
   Seek the Lord with love and joy! Let no mind of grief annoy, And come before His presence with a song.

2. Know ye that the Lord is God! Praise His holy name!
   Know ye that the Lord is God! Praise His holy name!
   For He made us and will keep Faithful watch o'er all His sheep: Dear Shepherd of the flock and fold above.

CHORUS.
Oh, be joyful! Shout a-loud for joy! Oh, be joyful, Shout a-loud for joy!

3 Enter in His gates with thanks!
   And His courts with praise!
  Enter in His gates with thanks!
   And His courts with praise!
  Poor return our hearts can give
  For the blessings we receive:
  O! ever may our voices sing His praise.

4 O! how gracious is the Lord,
   Ever good and kind!
  Sing His praise with one accord!
   Joined in heart and mind.
  For His mercy's ever sure,
  And His truth will still endure;
  O! shout aloud for joy of such a God.

24. The Grand Old Story.

H. BONAR. Arr. from DONIZETTI. By per.

1. Come and hear the grand old sto-ry, Sto-ry of a-ges past;
   All earth's annals far surpassing, One that shall ev-er last.

REFRAIN.

No-blest, tru-est, old-est; New-est, fair-est, rar-est;

Sweet-est, sad-dest, glad-dest That the world has known.

2 Christ, the Father's Son eternal,
  Once was born Son of man;
  He, who never knew beginning,
  Here earthly life began. REFRAIN.

3 Here in David's lowly city,
  Tenant of manger bed,
  Child of everlasting ages,
  Jesus lays His head. REFRAIN.

26. Soldiers of the Cross! Arise.

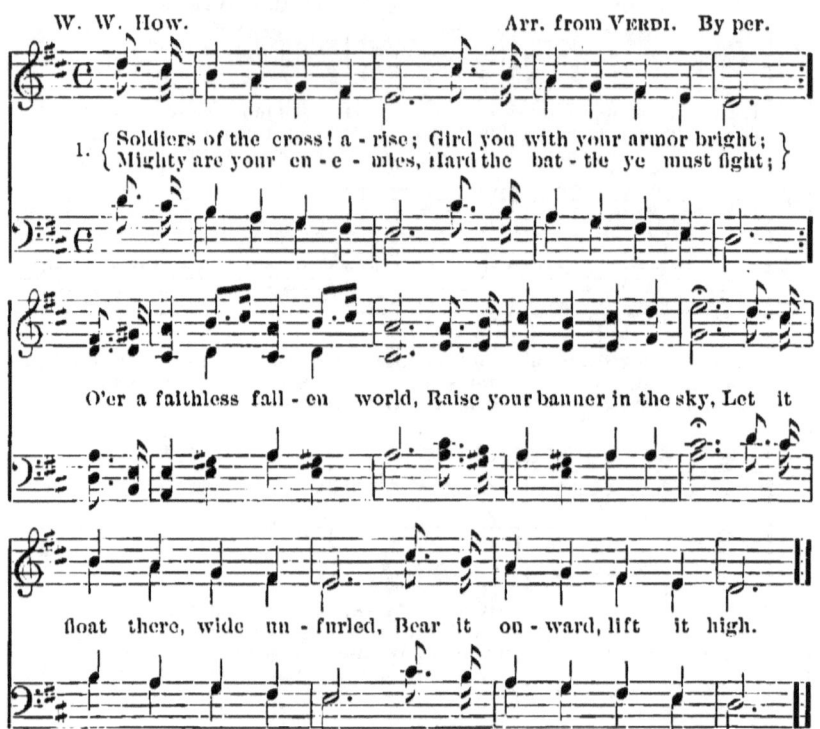

W. W. How. Arr. from VERDI. By per.

1. Soldiers of the cross! a-rise; Gird you with your armor bright;
Mighty are your en-e-mies, Hard the bat-tle ye must fight;
O'er a faithless fall-en world, Raise your banner in the sky, Let it float there, wide un-furled, Bear it on-ward, lift it high.

2 'Mid the homes of want and woe,
   Strangers to the living word,
Let the Saviour's herald go,
   Let the voice of hope be heard;
To the weary and the worn,
   Tell of realms where sorrows cease;
To the outcast and forlorn,
   Speak of mercy, grace, and peace.

3 Guard the helpless, seek the strayed,
   Comfort troubles, banish grief;
With the Spirit's sword arrayed,
   Scatter sin and unbelief:
Be the banner still unfurled,
   Bear it bravely still abroad,
Till the kingdoms of the world
   Are the kingdoms of the Lord.

32. Hitherto and Henceforth.

F. R. HAVERGAL. KARL REDEN. By per.

1. Hitherto the Lord hath helped us, Guiding all the way; Henceforth let us trust Him fully, Trust Him all the day.

REFRAIN.
Hitherto, Hitherto, Hitherto the Lord hath helped us, Guiding all the way, all the way; Let us trust Him, trust Him fully.

2 Hitherto the Lord hath loved us,
Caring for His own;
Henceforth let us love Him better,
Live for Him alone. REF.

3 Hitherto the Lord hath blessed us,
Crowning all our days;
Henceforth let us live and bless Him,
Live to show His praise. REF.

35. Wandering Sheep.

KARL REDEN. By per.

1. I was a wand'ring sheep; I did not love the fold; I did not love my Shepherd's voice, I would not be con-troll'd.
2. The Shepherd sought his sheep, The Father sought his child; They fol-lowed me o'er vale and hill, O'er des-erts waste and wild?
3. They spoke in tender love, They raised my drooping head; They gen-tly closed my bleed-ing wounds, My fainting soul they fed;

CHORUS.

I was a way-ward child; I did not love my home; I did not love my Father's voice, I loved a-far to roam.
They found me nigh to death, Famished, and faint, and lone; They bound me with the bands of love, They saved the wand'ring one.
They washed my filth a-way, They made me clean and fair; They brought me to my home in peace, The long-sought wander-er.

4 Jesus my Shepherd is;
  'T was He that loved my soul,
  'Twas He that washed me in His blood,
  'Twas He that made me whole;
  'T was He that sought the lost,
  That found the wand'ring sheep;
  'T was He that brought me to the fold,
  'Tis He that still doth keep.

5 No more a wand'ring sheep,
  I love to be controll'd;
  I love my tender Shepherd's voice,
  I love the peaceful fold;
  No more a wayward child,
  I seek no more to roam;
  I love my heav'nly Father's voice,
  I love, I love His home.

37. Jesus at Nain.

Mrs. E. H. Morse.   C. C. Converse. By per.

1. To the place of graves, a weeping train Is wending sad and slow; 'T is a wid-ow's on-ly son who is dead; To his bur-ial forth they go, Oh, what a wail from the mother's heart, Is that which breaks on the ear Of Je-sus, as pas-sing His journey on, the ci-ty of Nain draws near.

2 Her head bent low with its weight of woe,
   She sees not the Saviour's face,
Nor dreams of its look of pitying love,
   Betok'ning marv'lous grace.
But soft to her heart comes His tender voice,
   "Weep not," and she lifts her head;
Then gently laying His hand on the bier,
   He speaks to the silent dead.

3 "Young man, arise!" Oh, wondrous pow'r!
   The dead is the living now!
Then comes a light to his death-dimmed eye,
   A flush to His pallid brow.
They part once more, those cold, still lips;
   He speaks, while all who hear
With wonder gaze, and rev'rent say,
   "Of a surety, God is here."

39. Take thy Cross.

J. POLLARD.   LESTA VESE. By per.

1. Broth-er, take thy cross and bear it, Dark and heav-y tho' it be;
2. Broth-er, take thy cross of sor-row; Bear the heav-y weight of pain;
3. Broth-er, take thy cross and fol-low Je-sus thro' the shad-ows dim;
4. Broth-er, take thy cross; for Je-sus Gives thee strength its weight to bear;

Je - sus His com-mand has giv - en, Take thy cross and fol-low Me.
Je - sus bent 'neath such a bur - den, Why should such as thou complain.
Thou wilt find thy bur - den ea - sy, If thou wilt de - pend on Him.
Trust Him in the time of sor - row, He will hear and an-swer pray'r.

CHORUS.

Take thy cross, Take thy cross, Take thy cross, whate'er it be;

Take thy cross, Take thy cross, Learn to bear it cheer - ful - ly.

40. The Little Straying Lamb.

2 And I, a little straying lamb,
    May come to Jesus as I am,
      Though goodness I have none;
    May now be folded to His breast,
    As birds within the parent's nest,
      And be His "little one."

3 Thus by this gracious Shepherd fed,
    And by His mercy gently led
      Where living waters run,
    My greatest pleasure will be this,
    That I'm a little lamb of His
      Who loves the "little one."

41. Jesus, Still Lead on.

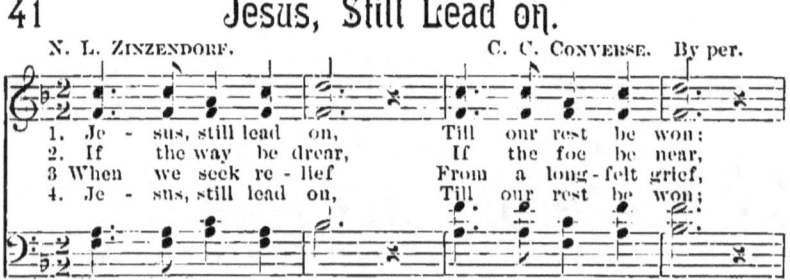

49. Be Our Light.

Rev. F. A. Faber. C. C. Converse. By per.

1. Dear Saviour, bless us ere we go: Thy word into our minds in-still; And make our luke-warm hearts to glow With low-ly love and fervent will.
2. The day is gone, its hours have run, And Thou hast taken count of all, The scanty triumphs grace hath won, The broken vow, the frequent fall.
3. Grant us, dear Lord, from evil ways, True absolution and release; And bless us more than in past days With purity and inward peace.

REFRAIN.
Thro' life's long day And death's dark night, O gentle Saviour, be our light.

4 Do more than pardon, give us joy,
   Sweet fear, and sober liberty,
   And simple hearts without alloy
   That only long to be like Thee. Ref.

5 For all we love, the poor, the sad,
   The sinful, unto Thee we call;
   Oh, let Thy mercy make us glad;
   Thou art our Saviour and our all. Ref.

50. I am Trusting Thee.

F. R. HAVERGAL. LESTA VESE. By per.

2. I am trusting Thee for cleansing,
   Cleansing in the crimson flood;
   Trusting Thee to make me holy,
   Make me holy by Thy blood. Cho.

3. I am trusting Thee to guide me,
   Jesus, Thou alone shalt lead,
   Every day and hour supplying,
   Every day and hour my need. Cho.

4. I am trusting Thee for power,
   Jesus, Thine can never fail;
   Words which Thou Thyself shalt give me,
   Blessed Jesus, must prevail. Cho.

52. Now I Have Found a Friend.

H. J. M. Hope. — Lesta Vese. By per.

1. Now I have found a Friend; Jesus is mine;—
   His love shall never end; Jesus is mine:
   Though earthly joys decrease,
   Tho' earthly friendships cease,
   Now I have lasting peace; Jesus is mine.

2. Though I grow poor and old, Jesus is mine;
   Though I grow faint and cold, Jesus is mine.
   He shall my wants supply,
   His precious blood is nigh,
   Naught can my hope destroy; Jesus is mine.

REFRAIN.
Jesus, Jesus, Jesus is mine, is mine; Jesus, Jesus, Jesus is mine.

3 When earth shall pass away,—
　Jesus is mine,—
In the great judgment day,—
　Jesus is mine.
Oh! what a glorious thing,
Then to behold my King,
On tuneful harp to sing,
　Jesus is mine. REF.

4 Father! Thy name I bless;
　Jesus is mine;
Thine was the sov'reign grace;
　Praise shall be Thine;
Spirit of holiness!
Sealing the Father's grace;
Thou mad'st my soul embrace
　Jesus, as mine. REF.

53. Pilgrim Song.

G. CRABBE.   C. C. CONVERSE. By per.

1. Pil-grim! burdened with thy sin, Come the way to Zi-on's gate;
2. Hark! it is the Bridegroom's voice, "Welcome, pilgrim! to thy rest!"
3. Ho-ly pil-grim! what for thee, In a world like this, re-mains?

There, till mer-cy speaks with-in, Knock, and weep, and watch, and wait:
Now with-in the gate re-joice, Safe, and sealed, and bought, and blessed:
From thy guard-ed breast shall flee Fear, and shame, and doubt, and pains:

Knock—He knows the sin-ner's cry; Weep—He loves the mourn-er's tears;
Safe—from all the lures of vice; Sealed—by signs the cho-sen know;
Fear—the hope of heav'n shall fly; Shame—from glo-ry's view re-tire;

Watch—for sav-ing grace is nigh; Wait—till heav'nly light ap-pears.
Bought—by love, and life the price; Blessed—the mighty debt to owe.
Doubt in cer-tain rap-ture die; Pain—in end-less bliss ex-pire.

54 Jesus, Meek and Gentle.

G. R. Prynne. C. C. Converse. By per.

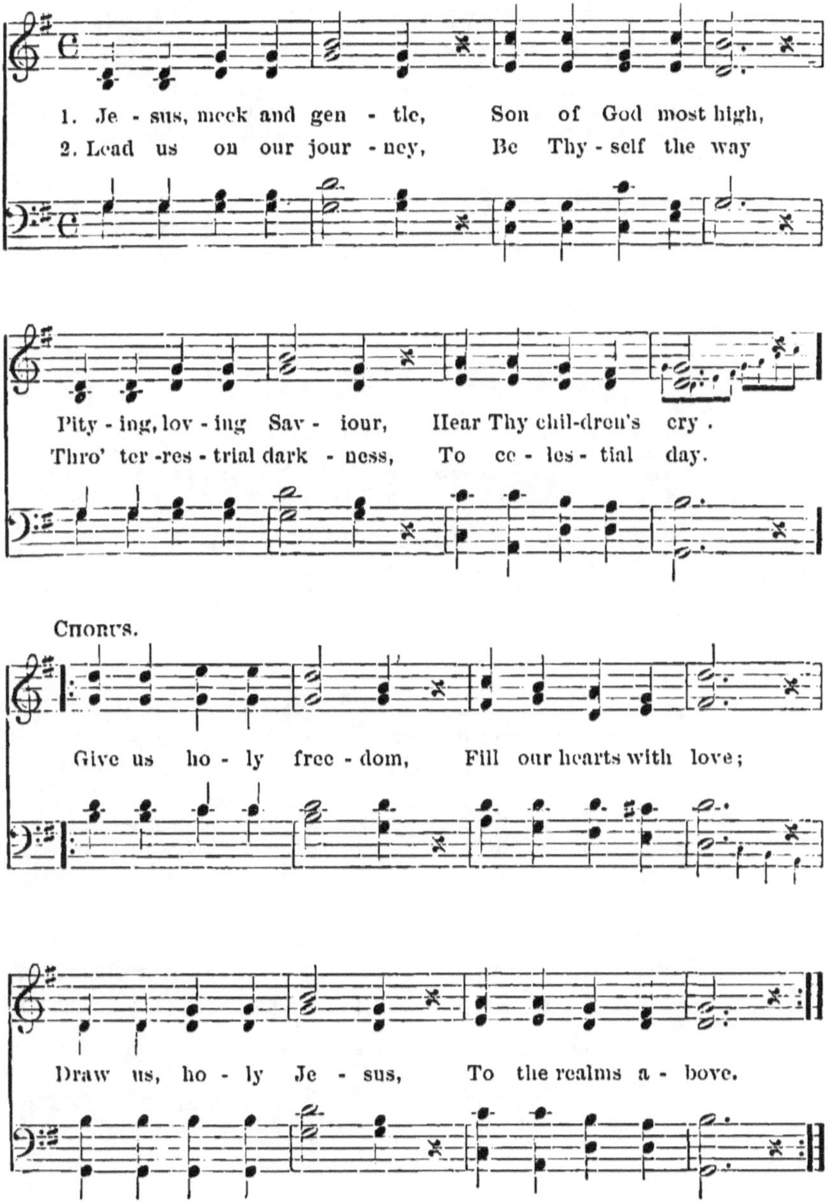

BEYOND THE RIVER.

We shall meet beyond the river, Meet to part no more.

58. Yet There is Room.

Rev. H. Bonar. C. C. Converse. By per.
DUET.

1. "Yet there is room!" The Lamb's bright hall of song,
With its fair glory, beckons thee along;

CHORUS.
Room, room, Yet there is room. Enter, Oh! enter now, enter now.
Room, room, Yet there is room. Enter, Oh! enter now!

2 Day is declining, and the sun is low:
The shadows lengthen, light makes haste to go. Cho.

3 The bridal hall is filling for the feast;
Pass in, pass in, and be the Bride-groom's guest. Cho.

4 It fills, it fills, that hall of jubilee:
Make haste, make haste; 't is not too full for thee. Cho.

5 "Yet there is room!" Still open stands the gate
The gate of love; it is not yet too late. Cho.

6 Pass in, pass in! the banquet is for thee;
That cup of everlasting love is free. Cho.

7 All heav'n is there, all joy! Go in, go in;
The angels beckon thee the prize to win. Cho.

8 Louder and sweeter sounds the loving call:
Come, ling'rer, come; enter that festal hall! Cho,

57

59. Something for Thee.

C. C. CONVERSE. By per.

1. Something, my God, for Thee— | Something for | Thee! ||
That each day's setting sun may bring Some penitential | of - fer- | ing. ||
In Thy dear name some kind - ness | done; ||
To Thy dear love some wan - d'rer | won— ||
Some trial meekly | borne for | Thee, || Dear | Lord, for | Thee. ||

2 Something, my God, for Thee— | Something .. for | Thee! | ||
That to Thy gracious throne may rise
Sweet incense from some | sacri- | fice; ||
Uplifted eyes, undimmed by | tears—
Uplifted faith, unstained by | fears, ||
Hailing each joy as | light from | Thee, ||
Dear | Lord, from | Thee. ||

3 Something, my God, for Thee— | Something .. for | Thee. ||
For the great love that Thou hast given—
For the dear hope of | Thee and | heaven, ||
My soul her first allegiance | brings, |
And upward plumes her heavenward | wings ||
Near- | er to | Thee— ||
Near- | er to | Thee. ||

60. I Gave my Life for Thee.

H. BONAR.   Arr. from WEBER. By per.

1. I gave my life for thee, my precious blood I shed, That thou might'st ransom'd be And quicken'd from the dead; I gave my life for thee; What hast thou done for me? what hast thou done for me? what hast thou done, hast done for me?

2 I spent long years for thee
   In weariness and woe,
That one eternity
   Of joy thou mightest know;
I spent long years for thee;
Hast thou spent one for me?

3 My Father's house of light,
   My rainbow-circled throne,
I left for earthly night,
   For wand'rings sad and lone;
I left it all for thee;
Hast thou left aught for me?

4 I suffered much for thee,—
   More than my tongue can tell,
Of bitt'rest agony;
   To rescue thee from hell;
I suffered much for thee;
What dost thou bear for me?

5 And I have brought to thee,
   Down from my house above,
Salvation full and free,
   My pardon and my love;
Great gifts I brought to thee;
What hast thou brought to me?

6 O let thy life be giv'n,
   Thy years for me be spent,
World fetters all be riv'n,
   And joy with suff'ring blent;
Give thou thyself to me,
And I will welcome thee!

BROTHER, BE FAITHFUL.

62 Awake! the Master now is calling us.

FANNY J. CROSBY.　　　　　JOHN R. SWENEY. By per.

1. A-wake! a-wake! the Master now is call-ing us; A-rise! a-rise! and
2. A cry for light from dying ones in heathen lands; It comes, it comes a-
3. O Church of God, extend thy kind, maternal arms, To save the lost on
4. Look up! look up! the promised day is drawing near, When all shall hail, shall

trust-ing in His word, Go forth, go forth! proclaim the year of ju-bi-lee, And
cross the ocean's foam; Then haste, O haste to spread the words of truth abroad For
mountains dark and cold; Reach out thy hand with loving smile to rescue them, And
hail the Saviour King; When peace and joy shall fold their wings in ev'ry clime, And

CHORUS.

take the cross, the blessed cross of Christ our Lord.　On, on, swell the
get-ting not the starving poor at home, dear home.
bring them to the shel-ter of the Sav-iour's fold.
"Glo-ry hal-le-lu-jah," o'er the earth shall ring.

On, on, on,

cho-rus;　On, on, the morning star is shin-ing o'er us;

Swell the cho-rus, on, on, on,

AWAKE! THE MASTER NOW IS CALLING US.

64. Take thy Staff, oh Pilgrim.

TEODORE TILTON. C. C. CONVERSE. By per.

1. Take thy staff, oh pilgrim, Haste thee on thy way; Let the morrow find thee Far-ther than to-day; If you seek the ci-ty Of the gold-en street, Pause not on the pathway, Rest not wea-ry feet.
2. In thy heav'nly journey, Press with zeal a-long; Rest-ing will but wea-ry, Run-ning make the strong. Wings that eagles car-ry, Bear them in their flight; So thy burden bears thee; Sure-ly then 't is light.
3. Haste! it hath been told thee, All things are thine own; Pass the pearl-y por-tals, Stand before the throne. Here the jour-ney end-eth, Here thy staff lay down, En-ter here thy mansion, Here re-ceive thy crown.

CHORUS.

Then haste, Oh, haste thee, pil-grim, on thy way, And let the mor-row find thee Still near-er than to-day.

65. He is Coming.

C. F. ALEXANDER.   Arr. from the German. By per.

1. He is com-ing, He is com-ing, Not as once He came be-fore:
   Wail-ing In-fant, Born in weakness, On a low-ly sta-ble floor;
   But up-on His cloud of glo-ry, In the crim-son-tint-ed
   sky, Where we see the gold-en sun-rise In the ros-y dis-tance lie.

2. He is coming, He is coming,
   Not as once He wandered through
   All the hostile land of Judah,
   With His foll'wers poor and few:
   But with all the holy angels
   Waiting round His judgment seat,
   And the chosen twelve Apostles
   Sitting crowned at His feet.

3. He is coming, He is coming,
   Let His lowly first estate,
   And His tender love, so teach us
   That in faith and hope we wait,
   Till in glory eastward burning,
   Our redemption draweth near;
   And we see the sign in heaven
   Of our Judge and Saviour dear.

66. Watching.

Mrs. E. H. MORSE.   C. C. CONVERSE. By per.

1. 'T was a watching group that the an-gels found When they came to herald Christ's
2. 'T is to watching souls that an an-gel comes With the voice of sins for-
3. And to watching ones will the an-gel say, When Christ shall come on His

WATCHING.

birth, And "Glo - ry to God on high," they sang, And loud-er the ech - o - ing cho-rus rang "Good will and peace on the earth, Good will and peace on the earth."
giv'n, When Christ is born in the heart's inn, And all its chambers are tuned with-in To mel - o - dies of heav'n, To mel - o - dies of heav'n.
throne, "Fear not, fear not; to you I bring Glad ti - dings of joy, the heav- en - ly King Has come to claim His own, Has come to claim His own.

67 To-day the Saviour Calls.

1. To - day the Sav - iour calls! O list - en now; With - in these sa - cred walls To Je - sus bow.
2. To - day the Sav - iour calls! For ref - uge fly; The storm of ven - geance falls; Ru - in is nigh.
3. The Spir - it calls to - day! Yield to His pow'r; O grieve Him not a - way; 'Tis mer-cy's hour.

69. Oh! Eyes that are Weary.

J. N. DARBY.   C. C. CONVERSE. By per.

1. O eyes that are wea-ry, and hearts that are sore, Look off un-to Je-sus, now sor-row no more! The light of His vis-age, it shineth so bright, That here, as in heav-en, there need be no night.
2. While look-ing to Je-sus, my heart can-not fear; I trem-ble no more when I see Je-sus near; I know that His pres-ence my safeguard will be, For "Why are ye troubled?" He saith un-to me.
3. Still look-ing to Je-sus, O may I be found, When Jor-dan's dark wa-ters en-compass me round: They bear me a-way in His presence to be; I see Him still near-er whom al-ways I see.
4. Then, then shall I know the full beau-ty and grace, Of Je-sus, my Lord, when I stand face to face; Shall know how His love went be-fore me each day, And won-der that ev-er my eyes turned a-way.

70

1 The Lord is my Shepherd; no want shall I know;
   I feed in green pastures, safe-folded I rest;
   He leadeth my soul where the still waters flow;
   Restores me when wand'ring, redeems when oppressed.

2 Through valley and shadow of death though I stray,
   Since Thou art my guardian, no evil I fear;
   Thy rod shall defend me, Thy staff be my stay;
   No harm can befall, with my Comforter near.

3 In presence of sorrows my table is spread;
   With blessings unmeasured my cup runneth o'er;
   With perfume and oil Thou anointest my head;
   O! what shall I ask of Thy providence more?

4 Let goodness and mercy, my bountiful God,
   Still follow my steps till I meet Thee above;
   I seek, by the path which my forefathers trod
   Through land of their sojourn, Thy kingdom of love.

                                     JAMES MONTGOMERY.

71. Courage, Brother!

NORMAN MACLEOD, D.D. — SIR ARTHUR SULLIVAN.

1. Courage, brother! do not stumble, Tho' thy path be dark as night;
There's a star to guide the humble, Trust in God, and do the right.
Tho' the road be long and dreary, And the end be out of sight,
Foot it bravely, strong or weary, Trust in God, trust in God, trust in God, and do the right.

2 Perish "policy" and cunning,
Perish all that fears the light,
Whether losing, whether winning,
Trust in God, and do the right.
Shun all forms of guilty passion,
Fiends can look like angels bright;
Heed no custom, school, or fashion,
Trust in God, etc.

3 Some will hate thee, some will love thee,
Some will flatter, some will slight;
Cease from man, and look above thee,
Trust in God, and do the right.
Simple rule and safest guiding,
Inward peace and shining light,
Star upon our path abiding,
Trust in God, etc.

72. There Came Three Kings.

2 The Star shone brightly over-head,
　The air was calm and still,
O'er Bethl'hem fields its rays were shed,
　The dew lay on the hill:
We see no throne, no palace fair,
O where is the King? O where? O where?
O where is the King? O where?

3 An old man knelt at a manger low,
　A Babe lay in the stall;
The starlight played on the Infant brow,
　Deep silence lay o'er all:
A maid bent o'er the Babe in pray'r:—
O there is the King! O there! O there!
O there is the King! O there!

THE ANGELS' SONG.

old, From angels bending near the earth to touch their harps of gold.

4 And ye, beneath life's crushing load
Whose forms are bending low,
Who toil along the climbing way,
With painful steps and slow, —
Look now; for glad and golden hours
Come swiftly on the wing:
Oh, rest beside the weary road,
And hear the angels sing. CHO.

5 For lo, the days are hast'ning on
By prophet bards foretold,
When with the ever-circling years
Comes round the age of gold:
When Peace shall over all the earth
Its ancient splendors fling, [song
And the whole world give back the
Which now the angels sing. CHO.

74. Abide with Me.
H. F. LYTE. WILLIAM H. MONK.

1. A-bide with me! Fast falls the e-ven-tide, The darkness deepens; Lord with me abide! When other helpers fail, and comforts flee, Help of the helpless, O abide with me.

2. Swift to its close ebbs out life's little day; Earth's joys grow dim, its glories pass away; Change and decay in all around I see; O Thou, who changest not, abide with me.

3. I need Thy presence ev'ry passing hour; What but Thy grace can foil the tempter's pow'r? Who, like Thyself, my guide and stay can be? Thro' cloud and sunshine, Lord, abide with me.

4. I fear no foe, with Thee at hand to bless; Ills have no weight, and tears no bitterness; Where is death's sting? where, grave, thy victory? I triumph still, if Thou abide with me.

76. I Love the Sunday School.

Chorus for Infant Class. Arr. from the German. By per.

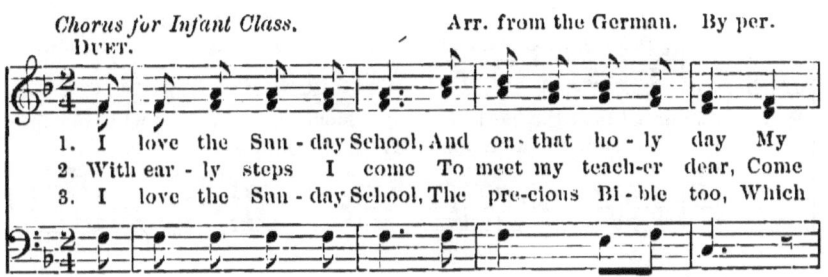

1. I love the Sunday School, And on that holy day My
2. With early steps I come To meet my teacher dear, Come
3. I love the Sunday School, The precious Bible too, Which

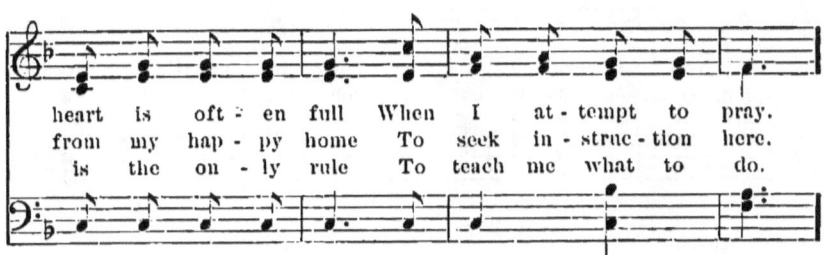

heart is often full When I attempt to pray.
from my happy home To seek instruction here.
is the only rule To teach me what to do.

CHORUS.

I love, I love, I love the Sunday School; I

love the Sunday School, I love the Sunday School.

77. The Blest Tidings.

Arr. from the German. By per.

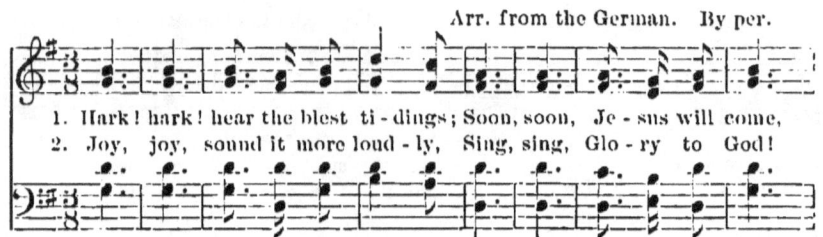

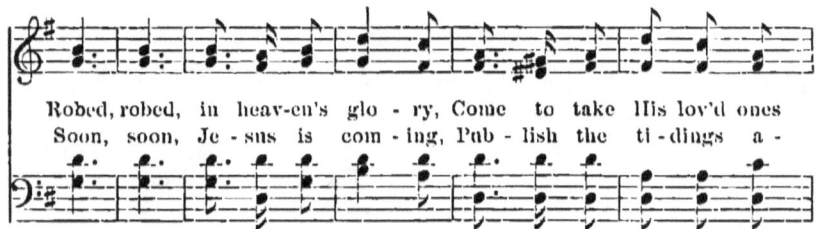

3 Bright, bright, seraphs attending,
   Shouts, shouts, filling the air;
  Down, down, swiftly from heaven,
   Jesus our Lord will appear.
     Yes, yes, O! yes,
  Jesus our Lord will appear.

4 Now, now, through a glass darkly
   Shine, shine, visions to come;
  Soon, soon, we shall behold them,
   Cloudless and bright in our home.
     Yes, yes, O! yes,
  Cloudless and bright in our home.

5 Long, long, we have been waiting,
   Who, who, love His blest name;
  Now, now, we are delighting,
   Jesus is near to proclaim.
     Yes, yes, O! yes,
  Jesus is near to proclaim.

6 Still, still, rest on the promise,
   Cling, cling, fast to His word;
  Wait, wait, if He should tarry,
   Patiently wait for the Lord.
     Yes, yes, O! yes,
  Patiently wait for the Lord.

79. Are you going to Jesus?

3 When at night by the pillow,
   We in penitence bow,
  List! His voice in mercy,
   Calling, "Come, sinner now." CHO.

4 When we cross the dark river,
   Calm and peaceful 't will be.
  If we hear Him calling,
   Calling, "Come unto me." CHO.

82. Tarry not Here.

By E. C. REVONS.

1. We are trav-el-ers here be-low, On-ward, joy-ful-ly still we go;
2. Oh! the light of that sky se-rene, Mortal vision hath nev-er seen;
3. Come and join us, a pil-grim band, Going home to our Fatherland;
4. Go-ing home to the fields of light, Go-ing home to our mansions right

On-ly pil-grims on earth we roam, Je-sus will gather us home.
Strains no mor-tal on earth can hear, Ech-o sweet melo-dy there.
Crowns of joy, so di-vine-ly fair, Je-sus will give us all there.
Oh, how hap-py we all shall be, Je-sus in heaven to see.

CHORUS.
On-ward! On-ward! Tar-ry not, Tar-ry not, tar-ry not here!
On-ward! On-ward! Tar-ry not, tar-ry not here.

83. God is Love.

J. BOWRING.   Arr. from the German. By per.

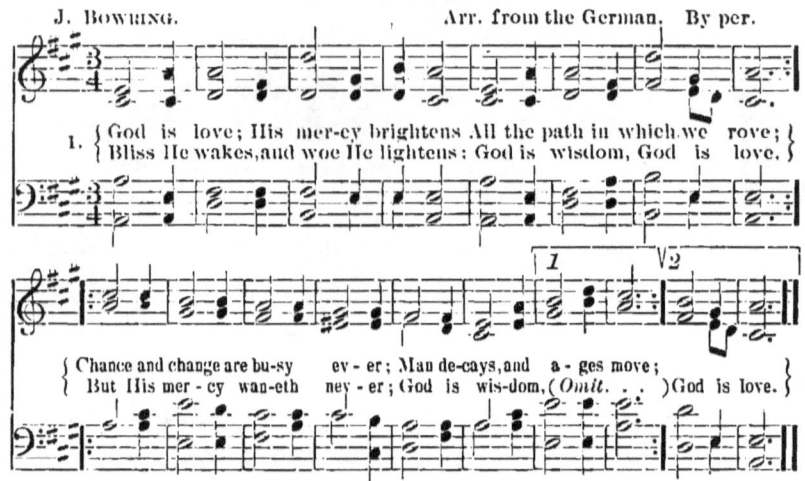

1. God is love; His mer-cy brightens All the path in which we rove;
Bliss He wakes, and woe He lightens: God is wisdom, God is love.

Chance and change are bu-sy ev - er; Man de-cays, and a - ges move;
But His mer - cy wan-eth nev - er; God is wis-dom, (Omit...) God is love.

2 E'en the hour that darkest seemeth
Will His changeless goodness prove;
From the cloud His brightness streameth:
God is wisdom, God is love.

3 He with earthly cares entwineth
Hope and comfort from above;
Everywhere His glory shineth:
God is wisdom, God is love.

84. With Joy we Hail the Sacred Day.

H. AUBER.   J. B. DYKES.

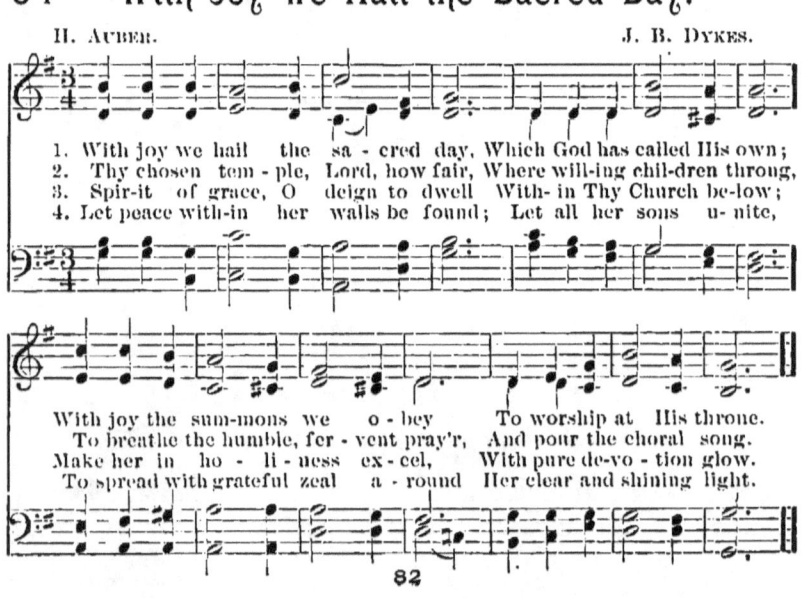

1. With joy we hail the sa - cred day, Which God has called His own;
2. Thy chosen tem - ple, Lord, how fair, Where will-ing chil-dren throng,
3. Spir-it of grace, O deign to dwell With-in Thy Church be-low;
4. Let peace with-in her walls be found; Let all her sons u-nite,

With joy the sum-mons we o - bey To worship at His throne.
To breathe the humble, fer - vent pray'r, And pour the choral song.
Make her in ho - li - ness ex - cel, With pure de-vo - tion glow.
To spread with grateful zeal a - round Her clear and shining light.

85. Benedictus.

Rev. John Ellerton.
E. J. Hopkins, Mus. Doc.

1. Sav-iour, a-gain to Thy dear Name we raise With one ac-cord our part-ing hymn of praise; We rise to bless Thee ere our wor-ship cease, And now de-part-ing, wait Thy word of peace.
2. Grant us Thy peace, up-on our homeward way; With Thee began, with Thee shall end the day; Guard Thou the lips from sin, the hearts from shame, That in this house have called up-on Thy Name.
3. Grant us Thy peace, Lord, thro' the coming night, Turn Thou for us its dark-ness in-to light; From harm and dan-ger keep Thy children free, For dark and light are both a-like to Thee.
4. Grant us Thy peace thro'-out our earthly life, Our balm in sor-row, and our stay in strife; Then, when Thy voice shall bid our con-flict cease, Call us, O Lord, to Thine e-ter-nal peace.

Children's Hallelujah.

CHILDREN'S HALLELUJAH.

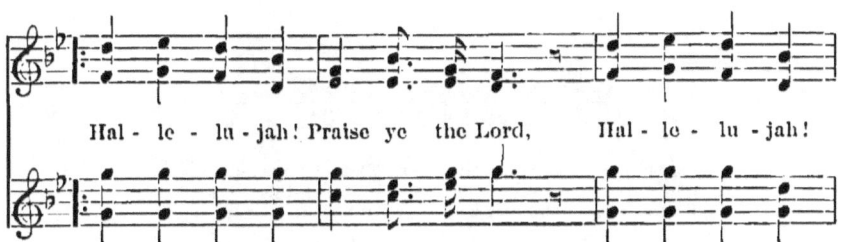

87. Better Than Thrones.

E. C. REVONS. By per.

1. There's nothing sweeter than the tho't, That I may see the Lord, If I but seek Him as I ought, And love His work and word.
2. Once in His arms the Sav-iour took Young children just like me, And bless'd them with a voice and look, As kind as kind could be.
3. And tho' to heav'n the Lord hath gone, And seems so far a-way, He hath a smile for ev-'ry one That doth His voice o-bey.

CHORUS.

I'd rath-er be the least of them That are the Lord's a-bove, Than
I'd rath-er be the least of them That shar'd that look and tone, Than
I'd rath-er be the least of them That He will bless and own, Than

wear a roy-al di-a-dem, And sit up-on a throne.

THE TWO SONGS.

90. Thy Will be Done.

CHARLOTTE ELLIOTT.   C. C. CONVERSE. By per.

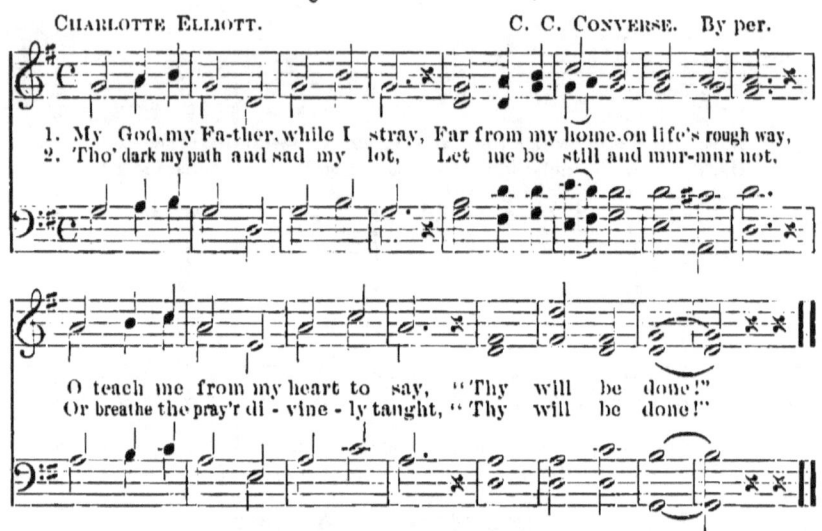

1. My God, my Father, while I stray, Far from my home, on life's rough way,
O teach me from my heart to say, "Thy will be done!"
2. Tho' dark my path and sad my lot, Let me be still and murmur not,
Or breathe the pray'r divinely taught, "Thy will be done!"

3 If Thou shouldst call me to resign
What most I prize,— it ne'er was mine:
I only yield Thee what is Thine;
"Thy will be done!"

4 Let but my fainting heart be blest
With Thy sweet Spirit for its Guest,
My God, to Thee I leave the rest;
"Thy will be done!"

5 Renew my will from day to day;
Blend it with Thine, and take away
All that now makes it hard to say
"Thy will be done!"

6 Then, when on earth I breathe no more
The prayer oft mixed with tears before,
I'll sing upon a happier shore:
"Thy will be done!"

91. The Only Refuge.

Tr. by C. WINKWORTH.   J. BARNBY.

1. We have no refuge; none on earth to aid us; Save Thee, O
2. Father, Thy name be praised, Thy kingdom giv-en; Thy will be

THE ONLY REFUGE.

Fa - ther, who Thine own hast made us; But Thy dear pres-ence will not leave them lone - ly, Who seek Thee on - ly.
done on earth as 'tis in heav - en; Keep us in life, for - give our sins, de - liv - er Us, now and ev - er.

92 The Pearl of Greatest Price.

J. MASON.   DONIZETTI.

1. I've found the Pearl of great-est price, My heart doth sing for joy;
2. Christ is my Proph-et, Priest and King; A proph-et full of light;
3. For He in-deed is Lord of lords, And He the King of kings.

And sing I must; for Christ is mine, Christ shall my song em - ploy.
My great High Priest be - fore the throne, My King of heav'n -ly might.
He is the Sun of right-eous-ness, With heal - ing in His wings.

4 Christ is my Peace; He died for me,
   For me He gave His blood;
And, as my wondrous Sacrifice,
   Offered Himself to God.

5 Christ Jesus is my All in all,
   My Comfort and my Love,
My Life below, and He shall be
   My Joy and Crown above.

93. Till He come.

E. H. BICKERSTETH.   LESTA VESE. By per.

1. "Till He come!" Oh, let the words Linger on the trembling chords; Let the "little while" between In their golden light be seen; Let us think how heav'n and home Lie beyond that "till He come!"

REFRAIN. (*to be sung after the D.C.*)
"Till He come!" "till He come!" Jesus! Jesus, Jesus come!

2 When the weary ones we love
  Enter on that rest above;
  When the words of love and cheer
  Fall no longer on our ear;
  Hush! be every murmur dumb,
  It is only "till He come!" REF.

3 Clouds and darkness round us press;
  Would we have one sorrow less?
  All the sharpness of the cross,
  All that tells the world is loss.
  Death, and darkness, and the tomb,
  Pain us only "till He come!" REF.

4 See! the feast of love is spread,
  Drink the wine and eat the bread;
  Sweet memorials, till the Lord
  Call us round His heav'nly board,
  Some from earth, from glory some,
  Severed only "till He come!" REF.

95. Festal Anthem.

MONTGOMERY.   C. C. CONVERSE. By per.

1. Ho-san-na! ho-san-na! ho-san-na! be the children's song. Ho-san-na! be the children's song. Ho-san-na! ho-san-na! ho-san-na in the high-est. high-est.
Ho-san-na! be the chil-dren's song, To Christ the children's King.

2. Ho-san-na! ho-san-na! ho-san-na! then our song shall be, Ho-san-na! then our song shall be, Ho-san-na! ho-san-na! ho-san-na in the high-est. high-est.
Ho-san-na! then our song shall be, Ho-san-na to our King.

FESTAL ANTHEM.

MY HEAVENLY HOME.

97. Voice of the New Year.

Mrs. E. H. Morse.   C. C. Converse. By per.

1. List! list! list! Oh, children, say, do you hear? There comes a sound of Christmas chimes, And the bells of the glad New Year, And the bells of the glad New Year.
2. Peace! peace! peace! Till all the air is a-float; And joy! joy! joy! Swells from each answering throat, Swells from each answering throat.
3. Hark! hark! hark! Is there not in the chiming bells, Another note to the list'ning heart That a beautiful secret tells, That a beautiful secret tells.

4 Yes! yes! yes!
   It whispers that this may be
   The gladdest of all New Years
   That heaven has sent to thee.

5 List! list! list!
   To the voice of this joyous hour,
   O sweet bells, ring it! O angels, sing it!
   The note of magical power.

6 Love! love! love!
   The gift of our God, most kind;
   Love first to Him — then to our own,
   Then, love to all mankind.

98. Come, ye thankful People, Come.

Rev. H. Alford.   Geo. J. Elvey.

1. Come, ye thank-ful peo-ple, come, Raise the song of Har-vest-home;
2. All this world is God's own field, Fruit un-to His praise to yield;
3. Come then, Lord of mer-cy, come, Bid us sing Thy Har-vest-home;

All is safe-ly gath-er'd in, Ere the win-ter storms be-gin;
Wheat and tares there-in are sown, Un-to joy or sor-row grown;
Let Thy saints be gath-er'd in, Free from sor-row, free from sin;

God, our Mak-er, doth pro-vide For our wants to be sup-plied;
Rip-'ning with a won-drous pow'r, Till the fi-nal Har-vest-hour;
All up-on the gold-en floor, Prais-ing Thee for ev-er-more;

Come to God's own tem-ple, come, Raise the song of Har-vest-home.
Grant, O Lord of life, that we, Ho-ly grain and pure may be.
Come, with all Thine an-gels, come; Bid us sing Thy Har-vest-home.

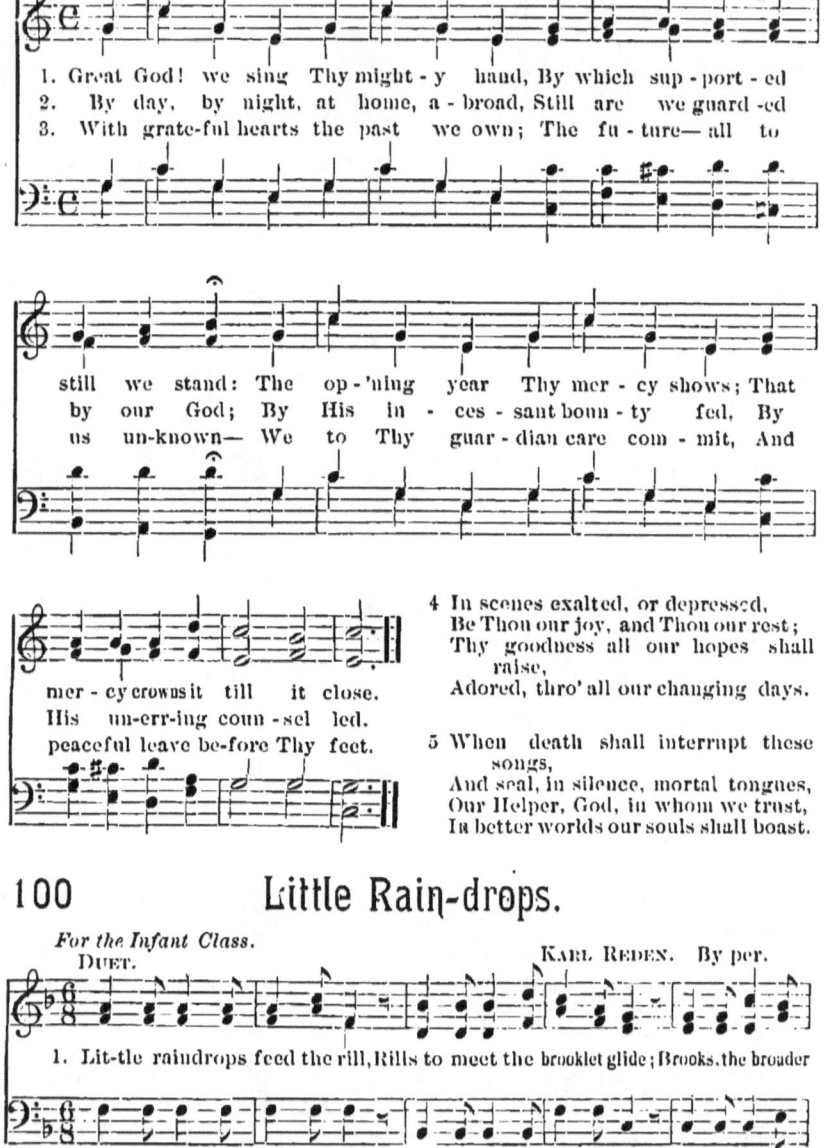

99. The Opening Year.

DODDRIDGE. LESTA VESE. By per.

1. Great God! we sing Thy might-y hand, By which sup-port-ed still we stand: The op-'ning year Thy mer-cy shows; That mer-cy crowns it till it close.
2. By day, by night, at home, a-broad, Still are we guard-ed by our God; By His in-ces-sant boun-ty fed, By His un-err-ing coun-sel led.
3. With grate-ful hearts the past we own; The fu-ture— all to us un-known— We to Thy guar-dian care com-mit, And peaceful leave be-fore Thy feet.

4 In scenes exalted, or depressed,
Be Thou our joy, and Thou our rest;
Thy goodness all our hopes shall raise,
Adored, thro' all our changing days.

5 When death shall interrupt these songs,
And seal, in silence, mortal tongues,
Our Helper, God, in whom we trust,
In better worlds our souls shall boast.

100. Little Rain-drops.

For the Infant Class.
DUET. KARL REDEN. By per.

1. Lit-tle raindrops feed the rill, Rills to meet the brooklet glide; Brooks, the broader

LITTLE RAIN-DROPS.

riv - ers fill. Rivers swell the ocean's tide, Rivers swell the ocean's tide.

2 So the dew-drops gathered here,
   Mites from willing childhood's hand,
   Shall those streams of bounty cheer,
   That with greenness clothe the land.

3 With that sea of love shall blend
   Which the gospel's grace doth pour;
   And the name of Jesus send
   E'en to earth's remotest shore.

101 Our Journey.

J. POLLARD. KARL REDEN. By per.

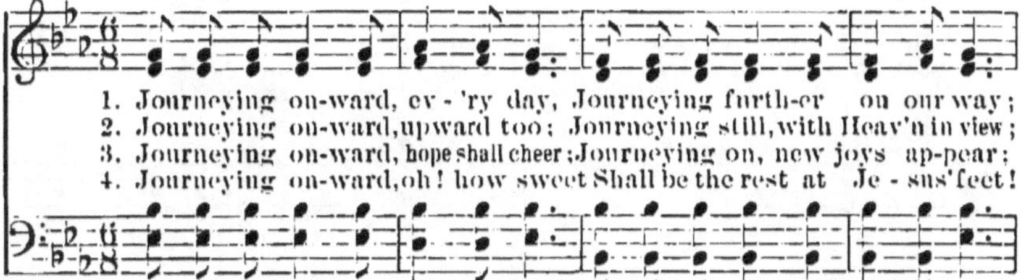

1. Journeying on-ward, ev - 'ry day, Journeying furth-er on our way;
2. Journeying on-ward, upward too; Journeying still, with Heav'n in view;
3. Journeying on-ward, hope shall cheer; Journeying on, new joys ap-pear;
4. Journeying on-ward, oh! how sweet Shall be the rest at Je - sus' feet!

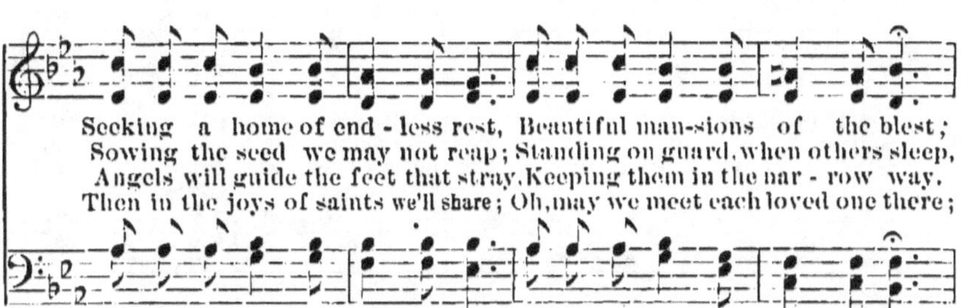

Seeking a home of end - less rest, Beautiful man-sions of the blest;
Sowing the seed we may not reap; Standing on guard, when others sleep,
Angels will guide the feet that stray, Keeping them in the nar - row way.
Then in the joys of saints we'll share; Oh, may we meet each loved one there;

Singing our songs of praise and love, Journeying to our home a - bove!
Jour-ney-ing on; a pil -grim band, Journeying to the bet- ter land!
Hopeful-ly wait -ing trusting still, Thus we may do our Master's will!
Soon shall our pilgrim days be o'er, Then shall we sin and toil no more.

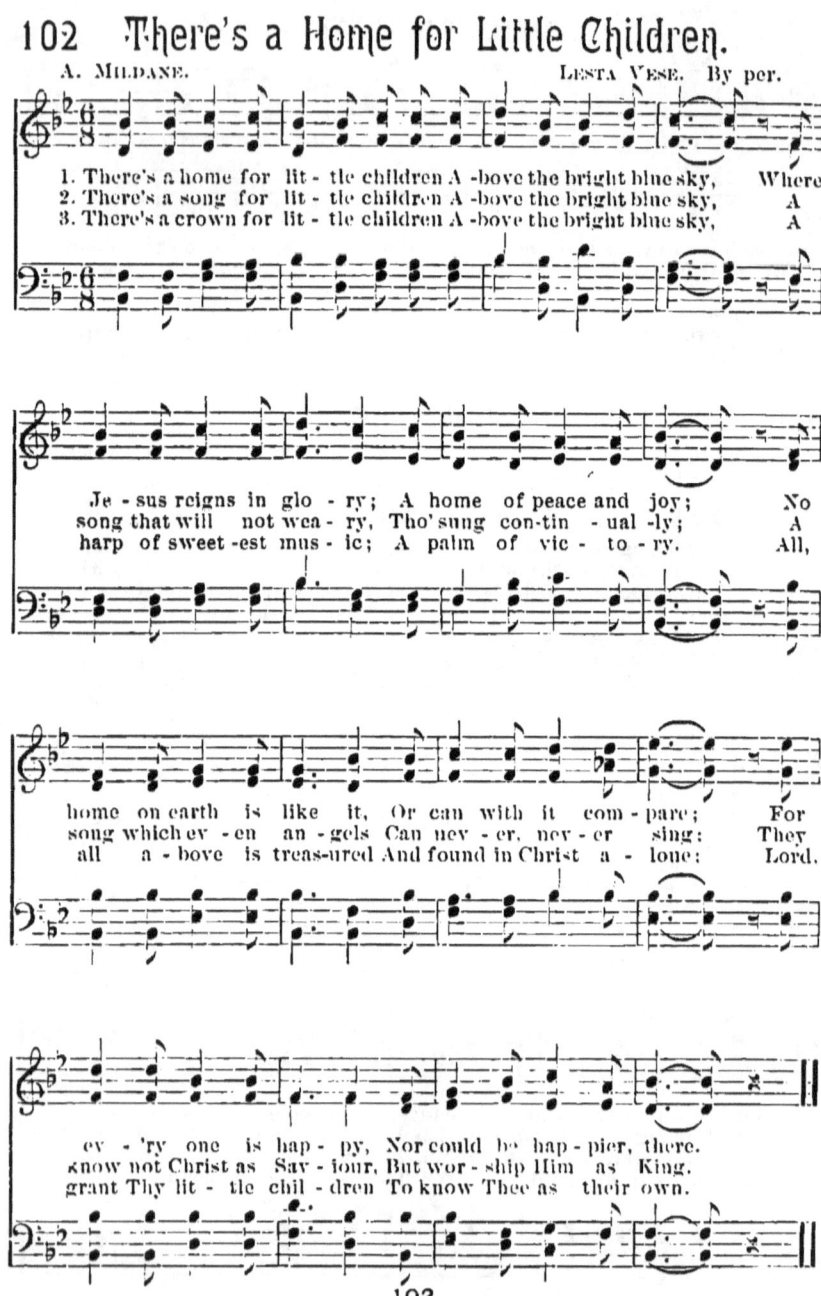

103. Sing of Jesus.

T. KELLY.   KARL REDEN. By per.

1. Sing of Je-sus, sing for ev-er, Of the love that changes nev-er.
2. With His blood the Lord has bought them; When they knew Him not, He sought them.
3. Thro' the des-ert Je-sus leads them, With the bread of Heav'n He feeds them.
4. There they see the Lord who bought them, Him who came from Heav'n, and sought them.

Who or what from Him can sev-er Those He makes His own?
And from all their waud'rings bro't them; His the praise a-lone.
And thro' all the way He speeds them To their home a-bove.
Him, who by His Spir-it taught them, Him they serve and love.

CHORUS.

Sing! Sing! Sing of Je-sus, sing for ev-er.

Sing! Sing! Sing of Je-sus for ev-er.

104 Ein' Feste Burg.

M. LUTHER. — M. LUTHER.

1. A might-y for-tress is our God, A bul-wark nev-er fail-ing;
Our help-er, He, a-mid the flood Of mor-tal ills pre-vail-ing;
For still our ancient foe Doth seek to work us woe; His craft and pow'r are great, And armed with cru-el hate; On earth is not His e-qual.

2. Did we in our own strength confide,
Our striving would be losing,—
Were not the right Man on our side,
The Man of God's own choosing:
Dost ask who that may be?
Christ Jesus, it is He!
Lord Sabaoth, His name,
From age to age the same;
And He must win the battle.

3. And tho' this world, with devils filled,
Should threaten to undo us,
We will not fear, for God hath willed
His truth to triumph through us:
The prince of darkness grim—
We tremble not for him;
His rage we can endure;
For lo, his doom is sure;
One little word shall fell him.

4. That word above all earthly powers—
No thanks to them—abideth;
The spirit and the gifts are ours,
Through Him who with us sideth:
Let goods and kindred go,
This mortal life also;
The body they may kill,
God's truth abideth still;
His kingdom is forever.

105 Let me come, Christ, close to Thee.

Rev. G. C. Rankin.   Karl Reden. By per.

1. Let me come, Christ, close to Thee, Christ my Sav - iour, Christ my King;
2. Let me suf - fer what I may, Let me tread on thorns of woe;
3. If Thou talk - est with my soul, Ev - 'ry oth - er voice may cease;

Stretch Thine arms so close to me, I can grasp Thy hands and cling.
So Thy feet are on the way, I am fear-less where I go.
All the world from pole to pole, All the u - ni - verse is peace.

CHORUS.

I am noth-ing if not Thine; Noth-ing if I can-not plead
That Thy sac - ri - fice di - vine Answers my im - mor - tal need.

4 Who can say he is alone,
   Though from all he walks apart,
   If he hears Thy blessed tone
   Fill the spaces of his heart?   Cho.

5 Thou art with me, O my Lord!
   Let that tender thought suffice;
   All my toil is but reward,
   All my sorrow, paradise!   Cho.

THE HAPPY SPIRIT-LAND.

Je - sus waits with outstretched arms, And bids His chil - dren "Come."

Saviour! I Follow On.

Rev. C. S. ROBINSON.   KARL REDEN. By per.

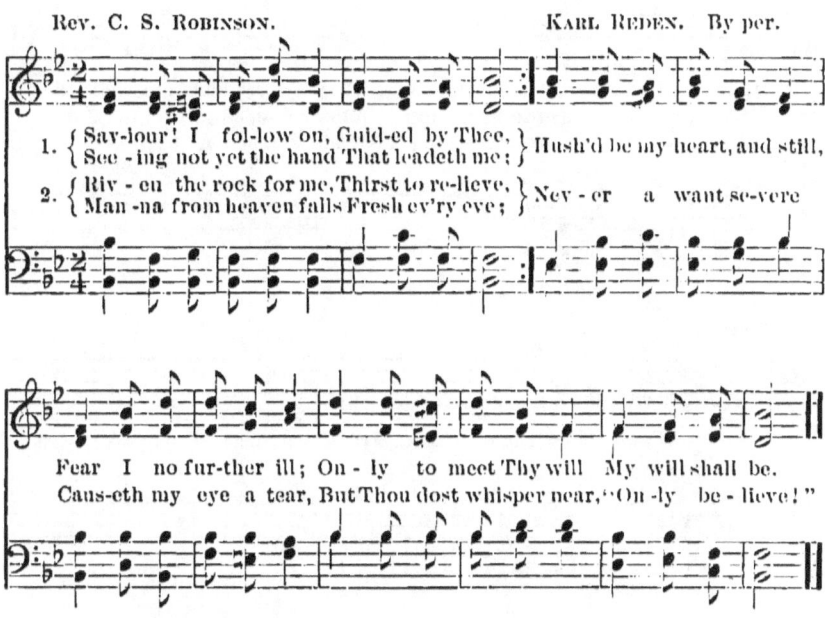

1. Sav-iour! I fol-low on, Guid-ed by Thee,
   See - ing not yet the hand That leadeth me;
   Hush'd be my heart, and still, Fear I no fur-ther ill; On - ly to meet Thy will My will shall be.

2. Riv - en the rock for me, Thirst to re-lieve,
   Man - na from heaven falls Fresh ev'ry eve;
   Nev - er a want se-vere Caus-eth my eye a tear, But Thou dost whisper near, "On - ly be - lieve!"

3 Often to Marah's brink
   Have I been brought;
Shrinking the cup to drink,
   Help I have sought;
And with the pray'r's ascent,
Jesus the branch hath rent—
Quickly relief hath sent,
   Sweet'ning the draught.

4 Saviour! I long to walk
   Closer with Thee;
Led by Thy guiding hand,
   Ever to be;
Constantly near Thy side,
Quickened and purified,
Living for Him who died
   Freely for me.

There is a Land.

G. Robins. Lesta Vese. By per.

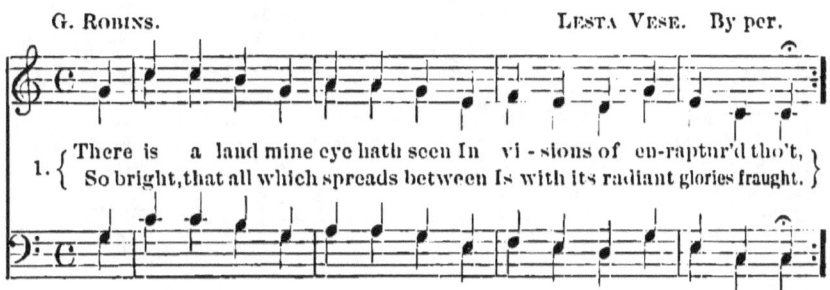

1. There is a land mine eye hath seen In vi-sions of en-raptur'd tho't,
So bright, that all which spreads between Is with its radiant glories fraught.

Chorus.

A land upon whose blissful shore There rests no shadow, falls no stain; There

those who meet shall part no more, And those long part-ed meet a-gain.

2 Its skies are not like earthly skies,
    With varying hues of shade and light;
  It hath no need of suns to rise
    To dissipate the gloom of night. Cho.

3 There sweeps no desolating wind
    Across that calm serene abode;
  The wand'rer there a home may find
    Within the paradise of God. Cho.

112 We Praise Thee, Heavenly Father.

Written and set to music by the Rev. J. D. HERRON.

1 We praise Thee, Heav'nly Father, (1 Tim. ii. 1)
    For token of Thy love: (1 St. John iv. 10)
  The blessed Intercession (Heb. vii. 22-25)
    Of Jesus, throned above. (Zech. vi. 13)
  He pleads for us the merit. (Heb. viii. 6)
    That every need supplies;
  All virtue we inherit. (Heb. viii. 10)
    Through His great sacrifice.

2 We call to Thy remembrance (Psa. xxv. 6; Isa. xliii. 25, 26.
    The Passion of Thy Son; (1 Cor. xi. 25. 26)
  His Resurrection, Triumph (Rom. viii. 34)
    O'er Death and Satan won. (Heb. ii. 14)
  For He our Priest hath entered (Heb. ix. 12)
    Within the Holy Place. (Heb. ix. 24)
  And there His Blood He sprinkles (Lev. xvi. 12-14)
    To claim Thy cleansing grace. (Heb. x. 14)

WE PRAISE THEE, HEAVENLY FATHER.

3 In majesty, O Father! (Psa. civ. 1, 2)
   Thou dwellest, clothed in light
Whose glory blinds the vision (2 Tim. vi. 16)
   Of our poor mortal sight.
But by the Blood of Jesus (Heb. x. 19, 20)
   The new and living Way,
We boldly seek Thy presence (Heb. x. 22)
   And worship Thee to-day. (Rev. iv. 11)

4 Therefore, O loving Father, (St. Matt. xxvi. 26-28)
   By holy bread and wine
We plead the Death of Jesus, (Rev. v. 6-8)
   The Sacrifice Divine.
Oh! by Thy Holy Spirit, (Rom. viii. 26, 27)
   Who intercedes below,
Give answer to our pleading, (Heb. x. 16, 17)
   And Thy best gifts bestow. (2 Cor. ix. 15) AMEN.

113 The Youthful Band.

KARL REDEN. By per.

1. We're marching to the promis'd land, A land all fair and bright;
   Come, join our happy, youthful band, And reach the plains of light.
2. The Saviour feeds His little flock, His grace is free-ly given;
   The liv-ing waters from the rock, And dai-ly bread from heav'n.

CHORUS.
Oh, come and join our youth-ful band, Our songs and tri-umphs share; We soon shall reach the promis'd land, And rest forev-er-more.

3 In that bright land no sin is found,
   But all are happy there;
And youthful voices there shall join
   With the glad angel choir.
      Oh, come and join, etc.

4 Our teachers kind do point the way,
   And guide our feet aright,
To those bright realms of endless day,
   Where Jesus is the light.
      Then come and join, etc,

114. Good Tidings.

KARL REDEN. By per.

1. Shout the tidings of salvation To the aged and the young;
2. Shout the tidings of salvation O'er the prairies of the West;
3. Shout the tidings of salvation Mingling with the ocean's roar;

Till the precious invitation Waken ev'ry heart and tongue.
Till each gath'ring congregation With the gospel sound is blest.
Till the ships of ev'ry nation Bear the news from shore to shore.

CHORUS.
Send the sound the earth a-round. Send the sound the earth a-round.
Send the sound, send the sound, The earth a-round.

4 Shout the tidings of salvation
　O'er the islands of the sea;
Till, in humble adoration,
　All to Christ shall bow the knee.
　　Send the sound, etc.

5 Shout the tidings of salvation
　Till the world shall hear the call;
And with joyous acclamation,
　Crown the Saviour Lord of all.
　　Send the sound, etc.

Easter Service.

The choruses in this service are intended for General, as well as Easter, use.

"SING WITH ALL THE SONS OF GLORY."
OPENING ANTHEM.

W. J. IRONS. C. C. CONVERSE. By per.

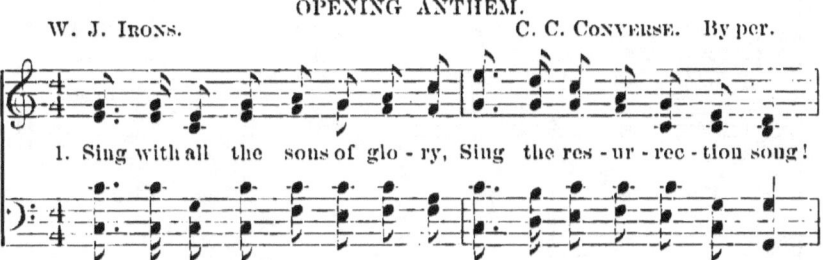

1. Sing with all the sons of glo-ry, Sing the res-ur-rec-tion song!

Death and sor-row, earth's dark sto-ry, To the for-mer days be-long;

All a-round the clouds are breaking. Soon the storms of time shall cease,

In God's like-ness man, a-wak-ing, Knows the ev-er-last-ing peace.

SING WITH ALL THE SONS OF GLORY.

2 Life eternal! heav'n rejoices,
   Jesus lives who once was dead;
   Join, O man, the deathless voices,
   Child of God, lift up thy head!
   Patriarchs from distant ages,
   Saints all longing for their heav'n.
   Prophets, psalmists, seers, and sages,
   All await the glory giv'n.
      Hallelujah! etc.

3 Life eternal! O what wonders
   Crowd on faith; what joy unknown,
   When, amidst earth's closing thunders,
   Saints shall stand before the throne!
   O to enter that bright portal,
   See that glowing firmament,
   Know, with Thee, O God immortal,
   "Jesus Christ, whom Thou hast sent!"
      Hallelujah! etc.

Prayer: *closing with the Lord's Prayer, all joining in it.*

RESPONSIVE READING.
1 Cor. 5: 7, 8; Rom. 6: 9–11; 1 Cor. 15: 20–22.

1 Christ, our Passover, is sacrificed for us.
2 Therefore let us keep the feast,
3 Not with old leaven, neither with the leaven of malice and wickedness;
4 But with the unleavened bread of sincerity and truth.
5 Christ, being raised from the dead, dieth no more;
6 Death hath no more dominion over him.
7 For in that he died, he died unto sin once:
8 But in that he liveth, he liveth unto God.
9 Likewise reckon ye also yourselves to be dead indeed unto sin,
10 But alive unto God through Jesus Christ our Lord.
11 Now is Christ risen from the dead,
12 And become the first-fruits of them that slept.
13 For since by man came death,
14 By man came also the resurrection of the dead.
15 For as in Adam all die,
16 Even so in Christ shall all be made alive.

ANGELS! ROLL THE ROCK AWAY.
DUET, SEMI-CHORUS, AND CHORUS.

Thomas Scott.   C. C. Converse. By per.

1. An - gels! roll the rock a-way; Earth, yield up thy might - y prey;
See, the Saviour leaves the tomb, Glow-ing with im - mor - tal bloom.
Hark! the wond'ring an - gels raise Loud - er notes of joy - ful praise;
Let the earth's re - mot-est bound Ech-o with the bliss - ful sound.

2 Saints, here lift your rev'rent eyes;
  Now see Him to glory rise
  In long triumph through the sky,
  Up to waiting worlds on high. Cho.

3 Heav'n opes its bright portals wide!
  Saviour! Conq'ror! through them ride;
  King of glory! mount Thy throne,
  Boundless empire is Thine own. Cho.

COME, YE SAINTS! LOOK HERE AND WONDER.

Thomas Kelly. CHORUS. C. C. Converse. By per.

1. Come, ye saints! look here and won-der; See the place where Je-sus lay;

He has burst His bands a-sun-der; He has borne our sins a-way:

Joy - ful ti - dings! joy - ful ti-dings! Yes, the Lord is ris'n to - day.

Joy - ful ti - dings! joy - ful ti-dings! Yes, the Lord is ris'n to - day!

COME, YE SAINTS! LOOK HERE AND WONDER.

2 Jesus triumphs! — sing ye praises;—
  By His death He overcame:
  Thus the Lord His glory raises;
  Thus He fills His foes with shame:
   ‖: Sing ye praises -- :‖
  Praises to the victor's name. REF.

3 Jesus triumphs! — countless legions
  Come from heav'n, to meet their King;
  Soon, in yonder blessèd regions,
  They shall join His praise to sing:
   ‖: Songs eternal :‖
  Shall through heav'n's high arches ring. REF.

CHRIST, THE LORD, IS RISEN TO-DAY.

ADDRESS.

ALL HAIL THE POWER OF JESUS' NAME.
CLOSING CHORUS.

E. PERRONET.  OLIVER HOLDEN.

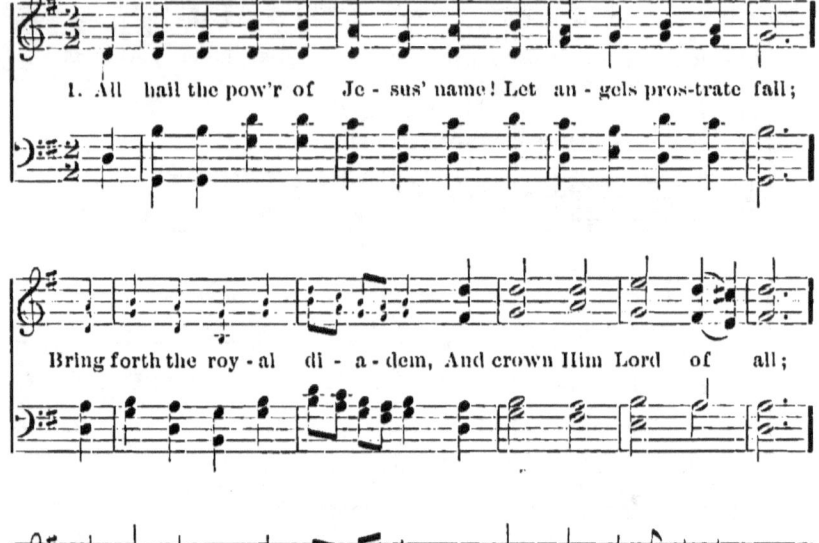

1. All hail the pow'r of Jesus' name! Let angels prostrate fall;
Bring forth the royal diadem, And crown Him Lord of all;
Bring forth the royal diadem, And crown Him Lord of all.

2 Crown Him, ye martyrs of our God!
Who from His altar call;
Extol the stem of Jesse's rod,
And crown Him Lord of all.

3 Ye chosen seed of Israel's race!
Ye ransomed from the fall!
Hail Him, who saves you by His grace,
And crown Him Lord of all.

4 Sinners! whose love can ne'er forget
The wormwood and the gall,
Go, spread your trophies at His feet,
And crown Him Lord of all.

5 Let every kindred, every tribe,
On this terrestrial ball,
To Him all majesty ascribe,
And crown Him Lord of all.

6 Oh! that, with yonder sacred throng,
We at His feet may fall;
We'll join the everlasting song,
And crown Him Lord of all.

BENEDICTION.

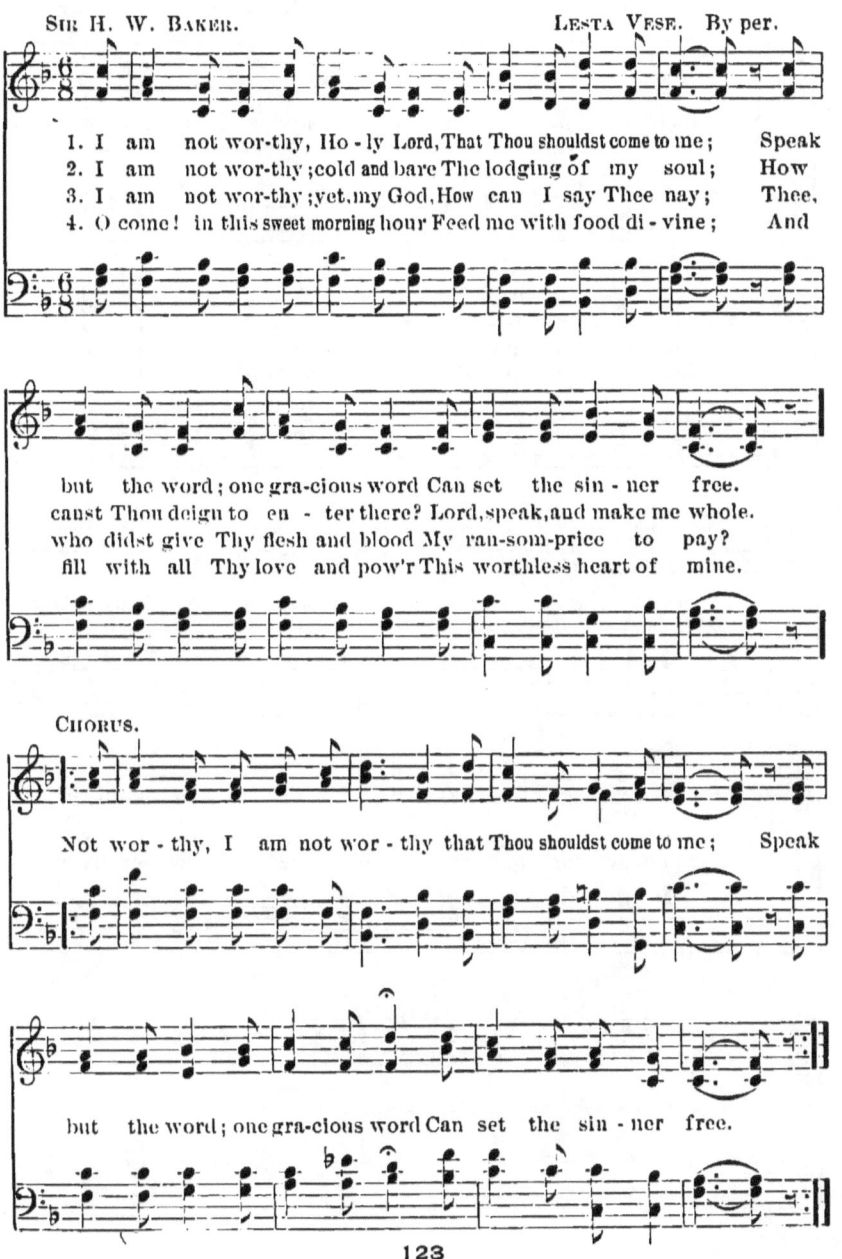

PILLAR OF CLOUD.

He is a pil-lar of fire by night, A pil-lar of cloud each day.

3 We're marching thro' a wilderness;
  Marching, marching;
We're marching thro' a wilderness,
  Beset on every side.
But the smitten rock will give
Healing draught that we may live;
He will all our sins forgive,
  And every want provide.

5 We're marching thro' a wilderness;
  Marching, marching;
We're marching thro' a wilderness,
  With Christ our beacon light.
He will lead us through the flood,
He will give us daily food;
He will save us by His blood;
  And keep us day and night.

118 Revive Us Again.

WM. P. MACKAY.   Arr. from the English.

1. We praise Thee, O God! for the Son of Thy love, For Je-sus who died and is now gone a-bove. Hal-le-lu-jah! Thine the glo-ry; Hal-le-lu-jah! a-men! Re-vive us a-gain.

2 We praise thee, O God! for thy Spirit of light,
  Who has shown us our Saviour and scattered our night.

3 All glory and praise to the Lamb that was slain,
  Who has borne all our sins, and has cleansed every stain.

4 All glory and praise to the God of all grace,
  Who has bought us, and sought us, and guided our ways.

121. I Could not do without Thee.

F. R. Havergal. Karl Reden. By per.

1. I could not do without Thee, O Saviour of the lost! Whose wondrous love redeemed me At such tremendous cost; Thy righteousness, Thy pardon, Thy precious blood must be My only hope and comfort, My glory and my plea.

2. I could not do without Thee, I cannot stand alone, I have no strength or goodness, No wisdom of my own; But Thou beloved Saviour, Art all in all to me, And perfect strength in weakness Is theirs who lean on Thee.

3 I could not do without Thee,
  For, O the way is long,
And I am often weary,
  And sigh replaces song.
How could I do without Thee?
  I do not know the way;
Thou knowest, and Thou leadest,
  And wilt not let me stray.

4 I could not do without Thee!
  For life is fleeting fast,
And soon in solemn loneness
  The river must be passed.
But Thou wilt never leave me;
  And though the waves roll high,
I know Thou wilt be with me,
  And whisper, "It is I."

OUR ROYAL CHRISTMAS GIFT.

Chorus.
He is our roy-al Christ-mas gift, And as we now be-lieve, We take the treas-ure to our hearts, And all His love re-ceive.

123 Lida. 7s.
C. C. Converse. By per.

1. Come said Je-sus' sa-cred voice, Come and make my paths your choice;
I will guide you to your home—Wea-ry pil-grim! hith-er come.

2. Hith-er come, for here is found Balm for ev-'ry bleed-ing wound,
Peace which ev-er shall en-dure—Rest e-ter-nal, sa-cred, sure.

124

1 Depth of mercy, can there be
Mercy still reserved for me?
Can my God His wrath forbear?
Me, the chief of sinners, spare?

2 I have long withstood His grace;
Long provoked Him to His face;
Would not hearken to His calls;
Grieved Him by a thousand falls.

3 Now incline me to repent;
Let me now my sins lament;
Now my foul revolt deplore,
Weep, believe, and sin no more.

126. Lord, in Mercy Hear us.

T. B. Pollock.
Sir A. Sullivan.

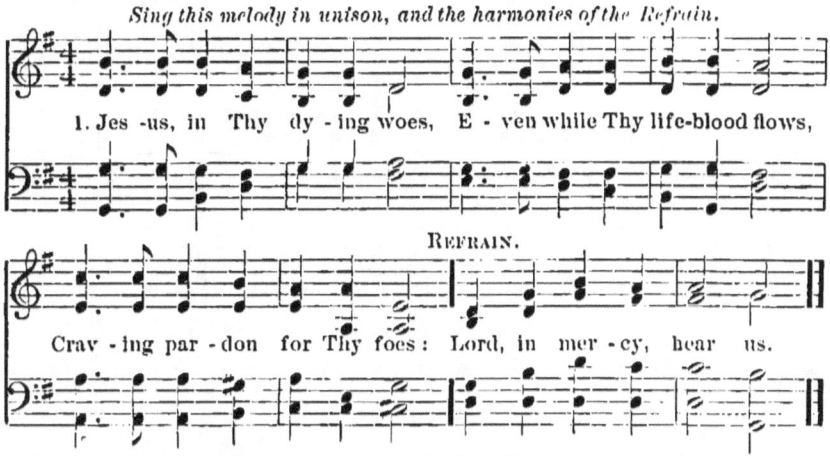

1. Jesus, in Thy dying woes,
E-ven while Thy life-blood flows,
Craving pardon for Thy foes:
Lord, in mercy, hear us.

2 Saviour, for our pardon sue,
When our sins Thy pangs renew,
For we know not what we do:

3 O may we, who mercy need,
Be like Thee in heart and deed,
When with wrong our spirits bleed:

Part II.

1 Jesus, pitying the sighs
Of the thief, who near Thee dies,
Promising him paradise:

2 May we in our guilt and shame,
Still Thy love and mercy claim,
Calling humbly on Thy name:

3 O remember us who pine,
Looking from our cross to Thine;
Cheer our souls with hope divine:

Part III.

1 Jesus, loving to the end
Her, whose heart Thy sorrows rend,
And Thy dearest human friend:

2 May we in Thy sorrows share,
And for Thee all peril dare,
And enjoy Thy tender care:

3 May we all Thy loved ones be,
All one holy family,
Loving for the love of Thee:

Part IV.

1 Jesus, whelmed in fears unknown
With our evil left alone,
While no light from heav'n is shown:

2 When we vainly seem to pray,
And our hope seems far away,
In the darkness be our stay:

3 Though no Father seem to hear,
Though no light our spirits cheer,
Tell our faith that God is near:

Part V.

1 Jesus, in Thy thirst and pain, [drain,
While Thy wounds Thy life-blood
Thirsting more our love to gain:

2 Thirst for us in mercy still;
All Thy holy work fulfil,
Satisfy Thy loving will:

3 May we thirst Thy love to know;
Lead us in our sin and woe
Where the healing waters flow:

Part VI.

1 Jesus,— all our ransom paid,
All Thy Father's will obeyed,
By Thy sufferings perfect made:

2 Save us in our souls' distress,
Be our help to cheer and bless,
While we grow in holiness:

3 Brighten all our heav'nward way,
With an ever holier ray,
Till we pass to perfect day:

Part VII.

1 Jesus,— all Thy labor vast,
All Thy woe and conflict past,—
Yielding up Thy soul at last:

2 When the death shades round us low'r
Guard us from the tempter's pow'r,
Keep us in that trial hour:

3 May Thy life and death supply
Grace to live and grace to die,
Grace to reach the home on high:

127. Thou Art Coming.

F. R. HAVERGAL.   C. C. CONVERSE. By per.

1. Thou art com-ing, O my Saviour! Thou art coming, O my King! In Thy beauty all-re-splen-dent, In Thy glo-ry all-transcend-ent Well may we re-joice and sing!

CHORUS.
Coming! In the op'ning east, Herald brightness slowly swells! Coming! O my glorious Priest, Hear we not Thy golden bells?

2 Thou art coming! Thou art coming!
  We shall meet Thee on Thy way,
  We shall see Thee, we shall know Thee,
  We shall bless Thee, we shall show
  All our hearts could never say! Cho.

3 O the joy to see Thee reigning,
  Thee, my own beloved Lord!
  Ev'ry tongue Thy name confessing,
  Worship, honor, glory, blessing,
  Brought to Thee with glad accord! Cho.

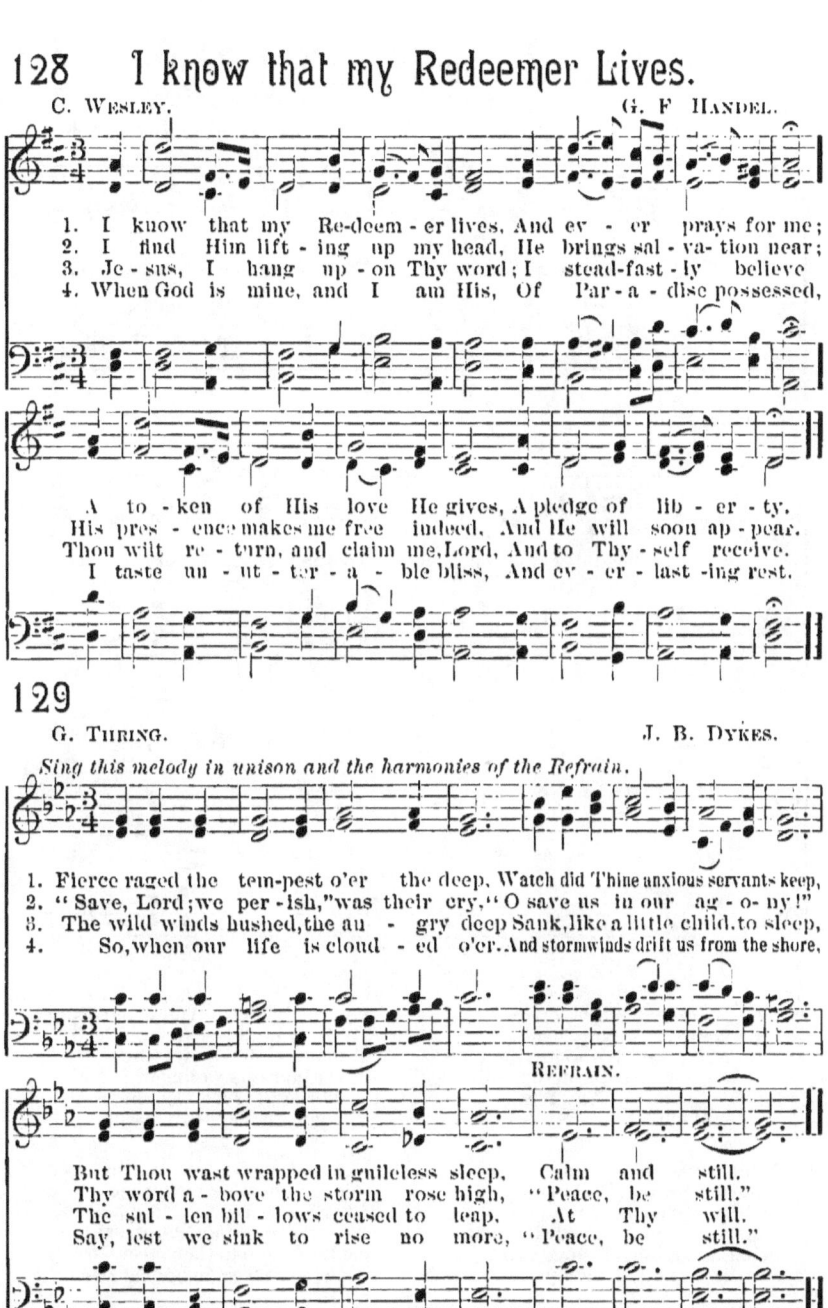

130. Hear Us, Jesus, as We Meet.

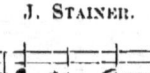
J. STAINER.

1. Thou to whom the sick and dy-ing Ev - er came, nor came in vain,

Still with healing words re-ply-ing To the wea-ried cry of pain;

Hear us Je-sus, as we meet, Suppliants at Thy mer-cy seat.

2 Every care and every sorrow,
  Be it great, or be it small,
Yesterday, to-day, to-morrow,
  When, where'er, it may befall,
Lay we humbly at Thy feet,
Suppliants at Thy mercy seat.

3 Still the weary, sick, and dying
  Need a brother's, sister's care;
On Thy higher help relying
  May we now their burden share,
Bringing all our off'rings meet,
Suppliants at Thy mercy seat.

4 May each child of Thine be willing,
  Willing both in hand and heart,
All the law of love fulfilling,
  Ever comfort to impart;
Ever bringing off'rings meet,
Suppliant to Thy mercy seat.

5 So may sickness, sin, and sadness,
  To Thy healing power yield,
Till the sick and sad, in gladness,
  Rescued, ransomed, cleansed, healed,
One in Thee together meet,
Pardoned at Thy judgment seat.

131. Evermore.

Tr. by J. M. Neale.
J. Stainer.

1. Of the Father's love begotten Ere the world began to be,
He is Alpha and Omega He the source, the ending He,
Of the things that are, that have been, And that future years shall see,
Evermore, and evermore.

2. At His word the worlds are framed; He commanded; it was done;
Heav'n and earth and depths of ocean In their three-fold order one;
All that grows beneath the shining Of the moon and burning sun,
Evermore, and evermore.

3. This is He whom seers in old time Chanted of with one accord;
Whom the voices of the prophets Promised in their faithful word;
Now He shines, the long expected; Let creation praise its Lord,
Evermore, and evermore.

4 O ye heights of heav'n adore Him;
Angel-hosts, His praises sing;
All dominions bow before Him,
And extol our God and King;
Let no tongue on earth be silent,
Ev'ry voice in concert ring;
Evermore and evermore.

132 He Is Gone.

A. P. STANLEY.   SIR A. SULLIVAN.

1. He is gone; a cloud of light Has received Him from our sight;
High in heav'n where eye of men Follows not, nor angels ken;
Thro' the veils of time and space, Passed into the holiest place:
All the toil, the sorrow done, All the battle fought and won.

2 He is gone; towards their goal
World and Church must onward roll:
Far behind we leave the past;
Forward are our glances cast:
Still His words before us range
Through the ages, as they change:
Whereso'er the truth shall lead,
He will give whate'er we need.

3 He is gone: but we once more
Shall behold Him as before;
In the heav'n of heav'ns the same,
As on earth He went and came.
In the many mansions there,
Place for us He will prepare:
In that world unseen, unknown,
He and we shall yet be one.

133. Lamb of God.

C. WESLEY.   BEETHOVEN.

1. Lamb of God, whose bleeding love We now re-call to mind, Send the answer from above, And let us mercy find; Think on us who think on Thee; Ev'ry struggling soul release; O remember Calvary, And bid us go in peace.

2 By Thine agonizing pain
   And bloody sweat, we pray,
By the dying love to man,
   Take all our sins away;
Burst our bonds and set us free,
   From iniquity release;
O remember Calvary,
   And bid us go in peace.

3 Let Thy blood, by faith applied,
   The sinner's pardon seal;
Speak us freely justified,
   And all our sickness heal;
By Thy passion on the tree,
   Let our griefs and trouble cease;
O remember Calvary,
   And bid us go in peace.

4 So from our sky, the night shall furl her shadows,
  And day pour gladness through his golden gates;
Our rough path leads to flower-enamelled meadows
  Where joy our coming waits.

5 Let us press on in patient self-denial;
  Accept the hardship, shrinking not from loss,
Our guerdon lies beyond the hour of trial;
  Our crown, beyond the cross.

THINE FOR EVER.

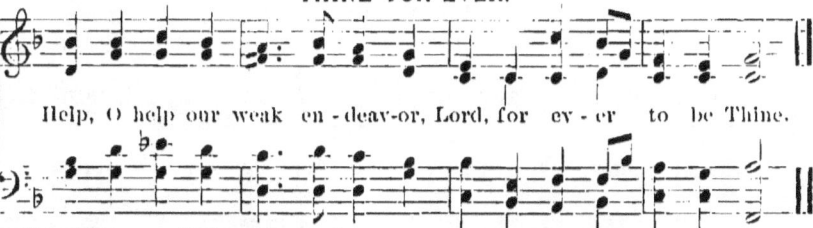

Help, O help our weak en-deav-or, Lord, for ev-er to be Thine.

2 Thine for ever, Thine for ever!
  Thine for ever may we be:
  May no sin or sorrow sever
  Us from union, Lord, with Thee.
3 Thine for ever, Thine for ever!
  Armed with faith and strong in
      Thee,

Ever fighting, fainting never,
  May we march to victory!
4 Daily in the grace increasing
  Of Thy Spirit more and more,
  Watching, praying without ceasing,
  May we reach the heav'nly shore!

136   He Standeth at the Door.

Written and composed by CLARENCE C. CONVERSE. By per.

1. Yield thy heart to Je-sus, Je-sus, Je-sus; Yield thy heart to Je-sus, He stand-eth at the door:

REFRAIN.
Yield thy heart to Je-sus, Je-sus, Je-sus, Yield thy heart to Je-sus, Bid Him en-ter in.

2 See Him standing, pleading, pleading, pleading;
  See Him standing pleading,
  He standeth at the door. REF.

3 If almost persuaded, wait not, wait not;
  If almost persuaded,
  He standeth at the door. REF.

4 Jesus is my Saviour, Saviour, Saviour,
  Jesus is your Saviour,
  He standeth at the door. REF.

137. Balerma.

R. Simpson.

1. Approach, my soul, the mercy seat, Where Jesus answers pray'r;
There humbly fall before His feet, For none can perish there.

2 Thy promise is my only plea,
   With this I venture nigh;
Thou callest burdened souls to Thee,
   And such, O Lord, am I.

3 Bowed down beneath a load of sin,
   By Satan sorely pressed,
By war without, and fears within,
   I come to Thee for rest.

4 Be Thou my shield and hiding-place,
   That, sheltered near Thy side,
I may my fierce accuser face,
   And tell him, Thou hast died.

5 O wondrous love to bleed and die,
   To bear the cross and shame,
That guilty sinners such as I,
   Might plead Thy gracious name.

138. In Thy Name Assembling.

T. Kelly. E. J. Hopkins.

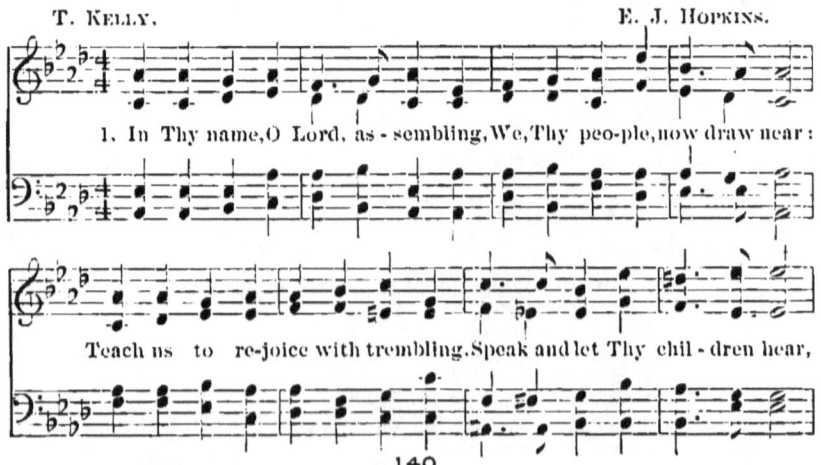

1. In Thy name, O Lord, assembling, We, Thy people, now draw near:
Teach us to rejoice with trembling. Speak and let Thy children hear,

IN THY NAME ASSEMBLING.

Hear with meek-ness, Hear Thy word with god - ly fear.

2 While our days on earth are lengthen'd,
   May we give them, Lord, to Thee;
   Cheer'd by hope, and daily strengthen'd
   May we run, nor weary be,
   Till Thy glory
   Without clouds in heaven we see.

3 There in worship purer, sweeter,
   Thee, Thy people shall adore;
   Tasting of enjoyment greater
   Far than thought conceived before;
   Full enjoyment,
   Full, unmixed, and evermore.

139 Come, Jesus, Redeemer.

RAY PALMER.   Arr. by LESTA VESE.

1. Come, Je-sus, Re-deem-er! a-bide Thou with me; Come, glad-den my spir-it that waiteth for Thee; Thy smile ev-'ry shadow shall chase from my heart, And soothe ev-'ry sor-row, tho' keen be the smart.

2 Without Thee but weakness, with Thee I am strong;
   By day thou shalt lead me, by night be my song;
   Though dangers surround me, I still every fear,
   Since Thou, the Most Mighty, my Helper, art near.

3 Thy love, Oh! how faithful! so tender, so pure!
   Thy promise, faith's anchor, how steadfast and sure!
   That love, like sweet sunshine, my cold heart can warm,
   That promise make steady my soul in the storm.

141. One with Thee.

J. G. Deck.   Sir A. Sullivan.

1. Lord Jesus, are we one with Thee? O height, O depth of love! Thou one with us upon the tree, We one with Thee above. Such was Thy grace, that for our sake Thou didst from heav'n come down, With us of flesh and blood partake, In all our mis'ry one.

2 Our sins, our guilt, in love divine
  Confessed and borne by Thee,
The gall, the curse, the wrath, were Thine,
  To set Thy members free.
Ascended now, in glory bright,
  Still one with us Thou art;
Nor life, nor death, nor depth, nor height,
  Thy saints and Thee can part.

3 O teach us, Lord, to know and own
  This wondrous mystery,
That Thou with us art truly one,
  And we are one with Thee.
Soon, soon shall come that glorious day,
  When, seated on Thy throne,
Thou shalt to wond'ring worlds display
  That Thou with us art one.

142 Hark! the Sound of Holy Voices.

C. WORDSWORTH. J. B. DYKES.

1. Hark! the sound of holy voices, Chanting o'er the crystal sea,
"Hallelujah, Hallelujah, Hallelujah, Lord, to Thee;"
Multitudes which none can number, Like the stars in glory stand,
Cloth'd in white apparel, holding Conqu'ring palms in ev'ry hand.

2 Marching with Thy cross, their banner,
 They have triumphed, following
Thee, the Captain of salvation,
 Thee, their Saviour and their King.
Gladly, Lord, with Thee they suffered;
 Gladly, Lord, with Thee they died;
And by death, to life immortal
 They were born and glorified.

3 Now they reign in heav'nly glory,
 Now they walk in golden light,
Now they drink, as from a river,
 Holy bliss and infinite;
Love and peace they taste forever,
 And all truth and knowledge see
In the beatific vision
 Of the blessèd Trinity.

143 O for the Pearly Gates.

C. F. Alexander.   C. C. Converse. By per.

1. The ro-seate hues of ear-ly dawn, The brightness of the day, The crim-son of the sun-set sky; How fast they fade a-way. O for the pearl-y gates of heav'n, O for the gold-en floor; O for the Sun of Right-cous-ness That set-teth nev-er-more.

2 The highest hopes we cherish here,
  How fast they tire and faint;
How many a spot defiles the robe
  That wraps an earthly saint.
O for a heart that never sins,
  O for a soul washed white;
O for a voice to praise our King,
  Nor weary day or night.

3 Here faith is ours, and heav'nly hope,
  And grace to lead us higher;
But there are perfectness and peace
  Beyond our best desire.
O by Thy love and anguish, Lord,
  O by Thy life laid down,
O that we fall not from Thy grace,
  Nor cast away our crown.

Arr. from WALLACE. By per.

1. Com-mit thou all thy griefs And ways in-to His hands,— To His sure trust and ten-der care, Who earth and heav'n commands; Who points the clouds their course, Whom winds and seas o-bey: He shall di-rect thy wand'ring feet, He shall pre-pare thy way. . . .

2. Thou on the Lord re-ly, So, safe, shalt thou go on: Fix on His work thy steadfast eye, So shall thy work be done. No prof-it canst thou gain By self-con-sum-ing care; To Him commend thy cause.—His ear At-tends the soft-est pray'r. . . .

148 Follow Me.

3 Take up thy cross, nor heed the shame;
   Nor let thy foolish pride rebel;
   Thy Lord for thee the cross endured
   To save thy soul from death and hell. Cho.

4 Take up thy cross and follow Christ,
   Nor think till death to lay it down;
   For only he who bears the cross
   May hope to wear the glorious crown. Cho.

149 Sing, my Tongue, the Saviour's Glory.*

Tr. by E. Caswall.   C. Gounod.

1. Sing, my tongue! the Saviour's glory; Tell His triumphs far and wide;
Tell aloud the wondrous story Of His body crucified;
How upon the cross a victim, Vanquishing in death He died.

2 Such the order God appointed
When for sin He would atone;
To the serpent thus opposing
Schemes yet deeper than his own;
Thence the remedy procuring,
Whence the fatal wound had come.

3 Thus did Christ to perfect manhood
In our mortal flesh attain:
Then of His free choice He goeth
To a death of bitter pain;
He, the Lamb, upon the altar
Of the cross, for us was slain.

4 Lo, with gall His thirst He quenches!
See the thorns upon His brow!
Nails His hands and feet are rending!
See, His side is open now!
Whence, to cleanse the whole creation,
Streams of blood and water flow.

150 God's Wonders.

W. Cowper.   Beethoven.
S. S. Solo.

1. God moves in a mysterious way His wonders to perform;

* For S. S. use it is effective if only the air is sung.

GOD'S WONDERS.

He plants His footsteps in the sea, And rides up-on the storm.

2 Deep in unfathomable mines
   Of never-failing skill,
 He treasures up His bright designs,
   And works His sovereign will.
3 Ye fearful saints, fresh courage take;
   The clouds ye so much dread
 Are big with mercy, and shall break
   In blessings on your head.
4 Judge not the Lord by feeble sense,
   But trust Him for His grace;

Behind a frowning providence
  He hides a smiling face.
5 His purposes will ripen fast,
   Unfolding ev'ry hour;
 The bud may have a bitter taste,
   But sweet will be the flow'r.
6 Blind unbelief is sure to err,
   And scan His work in vain;
 God is His own Interpreter,
   And He will make it plain.

151 Jesus, Thou hast Bought Us.

F. R. HAVERGAL. Adapted by KARL REDEN. By per.

1. Jesus, Thou hast bought us, Not with gold or gem, But with
   With Thy blessing filling Each who comes to Thee. Thou hast
   Thine own life-blood, For Thy di-a-dem.
   made us willing, Thou hast made us free.
   By Thy grand redemption, By Thy grace divine, We are on the Lord's side; Saviour, we are Thine!

2 Not for weight of glory,
    Not for crown and palm,
  Enter we the army,
    Raise the warrior psalm;
  But for love that claimeth
    Lives for whom He died,
  He whom Jesus nameth
    Must be on His side. CHO.

3 Fierce may be the conflict,
    Strong may be the foe,
  But the King's own army
    None can overthrow;
  Round His standard ranging
    Vict'ry is secure;
  For His truth unchanging
    Makes the triumph sure. CHO.

152. Will you go?

Adapted by LESTA VESE. *By per.*

1. We are bound for the land of the pure and the ho-ly, For the home of the happy, the kingdom of love; O ye wand'rers from God, in the broad road of folly, Will you go, will you go to the E-den above?

CHORUS.
Will you go, will you go, to the king-dom of love, Will you go, will you go, will you go? ... will you go?

2 In that blessèd abode neither sighing nor anguish
Can be found in the fields where the glorified rove; [still languish,
O ye sin-burdened ones, who in sorrow
Will you go, will you go to Eden above? CHO.

3 We would have thee with us; O we would not forsake thee,
And we halt yet a moment as onward we move,
Will you trust in the Lord? In His arms He will take thee,
And will bear thee along to the E-den above. CHO.

155 Son of the Living God, O Call Us.

H. A. MARTIN. Adapted by KARL REDEN. By per.

1. { O, Rock of A-ges, one Foundation, On which the liv-ing Church doth rest,
   The Church, whose walls are strong salvation, Whose gates are praise, Thy name be blest. }

CHORUS.

Son of the liv-ing God! O call us Once and a-gain to fol-low Thee; And give us strength whate'er be-fall us Thy true dis-ci-ples still to be.

2 When fears appal, and faith is failing,
Make Thy voice heard o'er wind and wave. [prevailing
"Why doubt?"—and in Thy love
Put forth Thy hand to help and save.
Cho.

3 And if our coward hearts deny Thee,
In inmost thought, in deed, or word,
Let not our hardness still defy Thee,
But with a look subdue us, Lord.
Cho.

4 O strengthen Thou our weak endeavor
Thee in Thy sheep to serve and tend,
To give ourselves to Thee for ever,
And find Thee with us to the end. Cho.

156 Earth has Nothing Sweet or Fair.

J. SCHEFFLER.
Tr. by F. E. COX. Adapted. By per.

1. { Earth has noth-ing sweet or fair, Lov-ly forms or beauties rare,
   But before my eyes they bring Christ, of beauty source and spring. }

EARTH HAS NOTHING SWEET OR FAIR.

When the morning paints the skies, When the gold-en sunbeams rise. Then my Sav-iour's form I find Brightly im-aged on my mind.

2 When, as moonlight softly steals,
　Heav'n its thousand eyes reveals,
　Then I think: Who made their light,
　Is a thousand times more bright.

　Lord of all that's fair to see,
　Come, reveal Thyself to me;
　Let me, 'mid Thy radiant light,
　See Thine unveiled glories bright.

157　　

O. HOLDEN.　　　　　　　　　　　J. B. DYKES.

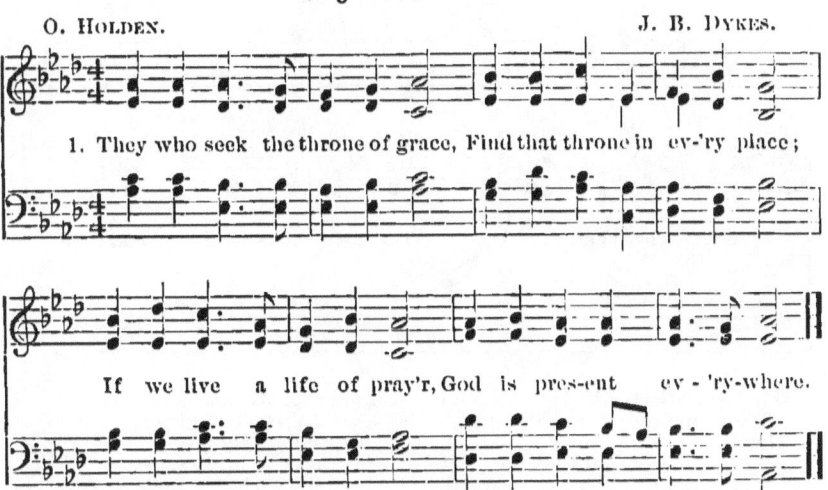

1. They who seek the throne of grace, Find that throne in ev-'ry place; If we live a life of pray'r, God is pres-ent ev-'ry-where.

2　In our sickness or our health,
　　In our want or in our wealth,
　　If we look to God in pray'r,
　　God is present everywhere.

3　When our earthly comforts fail,
　　When the foes of life prevail,
　　'Tis the time of earnest pray'r;
　　God is present everywhere.

158. Precious Saviour.

F. R. HAVERGAL. Adapted by KARL REDEN. By per.

1. O Saviour, precious Saviour, Whom yet unseen we love, O name of might and favor, All other names above:

CHORUS.
1,2,3. We worship Thee, we bless Thee, To Thee alone we sing; We praise Thee, and confess Thee Our holy Lord and King.

2 O bringer of salvation,
   Who wondrously hast wrought,
  Thyself the revelation
   Of love beyond our thought. Cho.

3 In Thee all fullness dwelleth,
   All grace and power divine;
  The glory that excelleth,
   O Son of God, is Thine. Cho.

4 O grant the consummation
   Of this our song above,
  In endless adoration,
   And evermore love: [Thee,
  Then shall we praise and bless
   Where perfect praises ring,
  And evermore confess Thee
   Our Saviour and our King!

2 Choose Thou for me my friends,
My sickness or my health;
Choose Thou my cares for me,
My poverty or wealth:
Not mine,—not mine,—the choice,
In things or great or small;
Be Thou my Guide, my Strength,
My Wisdom, and my All.   Thy way, etc.

162. Asleep in Jesus.

C. C. Converse. By per.

1. A-sleep in Jesus! bless-ed sleep, From which none ever wakes to weep, A calm and un-dis-turbed re-pose, Un-broken by the last .... of .... foes! ..

2 Asleep in Jesus! Oh! how sweet
To be for such a slumber meet,
With holy confidence to sing, [sting!
That death hath lost his venomed

3 Asleep in Jesus! peaceful rest,
Whose waking is supremely blessed;
No fear, no woe, shall dim that hour
That manifests the Saviour's pow'r.

163. This is not my Place of Resting.

H. Bonar. Arr. from Flotow. By per.

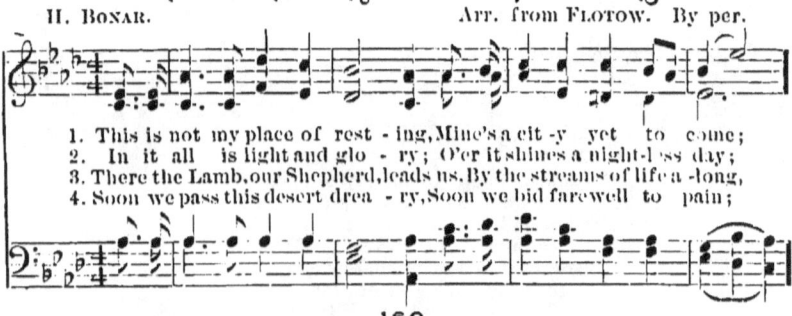

1. This is not my place of rest-ing, Mine's a cit-y yet to come;
2. In it all is light and glo-ry; O'er it shines a night-less day;
3. There the Lamb, our Shepherd, leads us, By the streams of life a-long,
4. Soon we pass this desert drea-ry, Soon we bid farewell to pain;

THIS IS NOT MY PLACE OF RESTING.

On-ward to it I am hast-ing, On to my e-ter-nal home.
Ev-'ry trace of sin's sad sto-ry, All the curse hath passed a-way.
On the freshest pastures feed us, Turns our sighing in-to song.
Nev-er more are sad and wea-ry, Nev-er, nev-er sin a-gain.

164. Be Kind to Each Other.

Adapted to F. ABT. By per.

1. Be kind to each oth-er, The night's com-ing on, When friend and when broth-er Will sure-ly be gone! Then, 'midst our de-jec-tion, How sweet to have earned The blest rec-ol-lec-tion Of kindness re-turned.

2 When day hath departed,
   And memory keeps
 Her watch, broken-hearted,
   Where all she loved sleeps,
 Let falsehood assail not,
   Nor envy disprove,
 Nor trifles prevail not,
   "Gainst those whom you love.

3 Nor change with the morrow,
   Should fortune take wing,—
 The deeper the sorrow,
   The closer still cling!
 Be kind to each other,
   The night's coming on,
 When friend and when brother
   Will surely be gone!

165 Brother, You may work for Jesus.

C. C. CONVERSE. By per.

1. Broth-er, you may work for Je-sus; God has giv-en you a place In some por-tion of His vine-yard, And will give sus-tain-ing grace. He has bid-den you to la-bor, And has prom-ised a re-ward—Ev-en joy and life e-ter-nal In the king-dom of your Lord.

2. Broth-er, you may pray to Je-sus, In your clos-et and at home, In the vil-lage, in the cit - y, Or wher-ev - er you may roam; Pray that He will send the Spir-it In - to some dear sin - ner's heart, And that in his soul's sal-va-tion You may bear some humble part.

3 Brother, you may sing for Jesus;
O how precious is His love! [ings,
Praise Him for His boundless bless-
Ever coming from above;
Sing how Jesus died to save you,
How your sin and guilt He bore,
How His blood hath sealed your par-
don,—
Sing for Jesus evermore.

4 Brother, you may live for Jesus,
Him who died that you might
live;
O! then all your ransomed powers
To His service freely give;
Thus for Jesus you may labor,
And for Jesus sing and pray;
Consecrate your life to Jesus—
Love and serve Him every day.

166. O for a Heart to Praise my God.

C. WESLEY. J. B. DYKES.

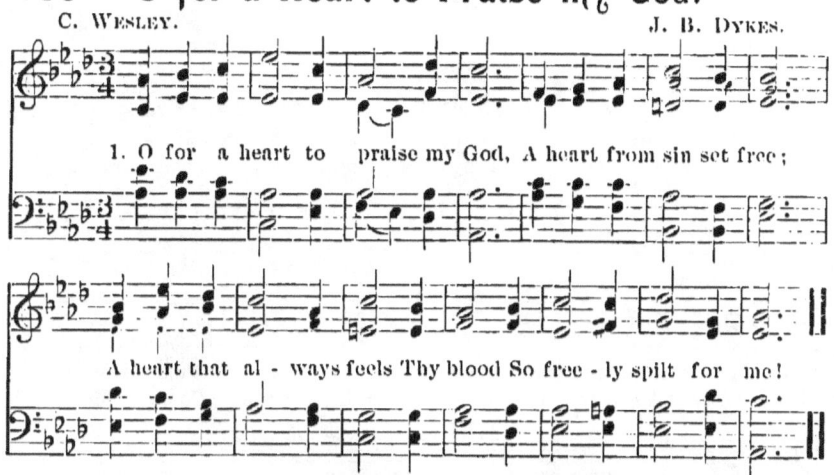

1. O for a heart to praise my God, A heart from sin set free;
A heart that al-ways feels Thy blood So free-ly spilt for me!

2 A heart resigned, submissive, meek,
My dear Redeemer's throne;
Where only Christ is heard to speak,
Where Jesus reigns alone.

3 A heart in every thought renewed,
And full of love divine;

Perfect, and right, and pure, and good,
A copy, Lord, of Thine.

4 Thy nature, dearest Lord, impart;
Come quickly from above;
Write Thy new name upon my heart,
Thy new, best name of love.

167 Praise God, from Whom all Blessings Flow.

GUILLAUME FRANC.

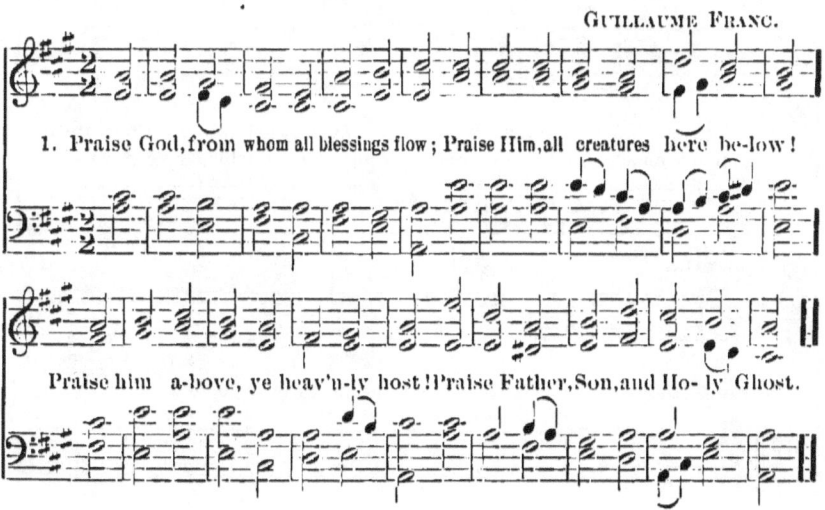

1. Praise God, from whom all blessings flow; Praise Him, all creatures here be-low!
Praise him a-bove, ye heav'n-ly host! Praise Father, Son, and Ho-ly Ghost.

170 Jesus, Whom Angel Hosts Adore.

H. BONAR. R. SCHUMANN.

1. Je-sus, whom an-gel hosts a-dore, Be-came a man of griefs for me;
2. The ev-er bless-ed Son of God Went up to Cal-va-ry for me;
3. Je-sus, whose dwelling is the skies, Went down in-to the grave for me;
4. 'Tis fin-ished all: the vail is rent, The wel-come sure, the ac-cess free;

In love, tho' rich, be-com-ing poor, That I thro' Him enriched might be.
There paid my debt, there bore my load, In His own bod-y on the tree.
There ov-er-came my en-e-mies, There won the glorious vic-to-ry.
Now then, we leave our ban-ish-ment, O Fa-ther, to re-turn to Thee.

171 We Praise Thee with Songs.

Mrs. MARGARET J. PRESTON.

1. We praise Thee with songs Of ho-ly ad-o-ra-tion: With lifted voice we
2. We praise Thee with psalms Of lowly ex-ul-ta-tion; While we adore the
3. We praise Thee with strains Of grateful ad-o-ration; Thro' Christ is giv'n sweet

would re-joice, To Thee praise belongs. The hosts on high Thy might declare. Earth
love that bore The thorns, not the palms! Thy mercy ev-'ry pathway crowns. Thy
rest in heav'n, The rest that remains: Then learn we here the lofty lay That

WE PRAISE THEE WITH SONGS.

chants Thy worship ev'rywhere; All things with glad accord Give praise to the Lord.
tender care each life surrounds,And hourly blessing prove How strong is Thy love.
never-more shall die away, Till we in glo-ry raise Our songs to His praise.

172 Blessing and Honor.

H. BONAR.   J. BARNBY.

1. Bless-ing and hon-or and glo-ry and pow'r, Wis-dom and
2. Past are the dark-ness, the storm,and the war; Come is the
3. Ev-er as-cend-eth the song and the joy, Ev-er de-

rich-es and strength ev-er-more, Give ye to Him who our
ra-diance that spar-kled a-far; Break-eth the gleam of the
scend-eth the love from on high, Bless-ing and hon-or and

bat-tle hath won, Whose are the kingdom, the crown,and the throne.
day with-out end; Ris-eth the sun that shall nev-er de-scend.
glo-ry and praise. This is the theme of the hymns that we raise.

4 Life of all life, and true Light of all
    light,   [bright,
Star of the dawning, unchangingly
Sun of the Salem, whose light is the
    Lamb,   [psalm!
Theme of the ever-new, ever-glad

5 Give we the glory and praise to the
    Lamb,   [the palm,
Take we the robe and the harp and
Sing we the song of the Lamb that
    was slain,
Dying in weakness,but rising to reign.

175. A Few More Years Shall Roll.

H. Bonar.   C. C. Converse. By per.

1. A few more years shall roll, A few more sea-sons come, And we shall be with those that rest, A-sleep with-in the tomb.
2. A few more suns shall set, O'er these dark hills of time, And we shall be where suns are not, A far se-ren-er clime.
3. A few more storms shall beat On this wild rock-y shore, And we shall be where tem-pests cease, And surg-es swell no more.

CHORUS.
Then, O my Lord, pre-pare my soul for that great day; O wash me in Thy precious blood, And take my sins a-way.

4 A few more struggles here,
  A few more partings o'er;
A few more toils, a few more tears,
  And we shall weep no more. Cho.

5 'T is but a little while
  And He shall come again,
Who died that we might live, Who lives
  That we with Him may reign. Cho.

179. Work for Little Ones.

CHANT.   LESTA VESE. By per.

1. There is no little child too small To | work for | God:
2. 'Tis not enough for us to give Our | wealth a- | lone;
3. The poor, the sorrowful, the old, Are | round us | still;
4. Father, oh give us grace to see A | place for | us,

There is a mission for us all From | Christ the | Lord.
We must entirely for Him live, And | be His | own.
God does not always ask our gold, But | heart and | will.
Where, in Thy vineyard, we for Thee May | la - bor | thus.

180. Come to Jesus, Little One.

LESTA VESE. By per.

1. Come to Je-sus, lit-tle one, Come to Je-sus now; Hum-bly at His
2. Seek His face without de-lay; Give Him now your heart; Tar-ry not, but,

gra-cious throne In sub-mis-sion bow. At His feet con-fess your sin;
while you may, Choose the bet-ter part. Come to Je-sus, lit-tle one,

Seek forgiveness there; For His blood can make you clean; He will hear your pray'r.
Come to Je-sus now; Hum-bly at His gracious throne In submission bow.

181 Jesus, Lover of my Soul!

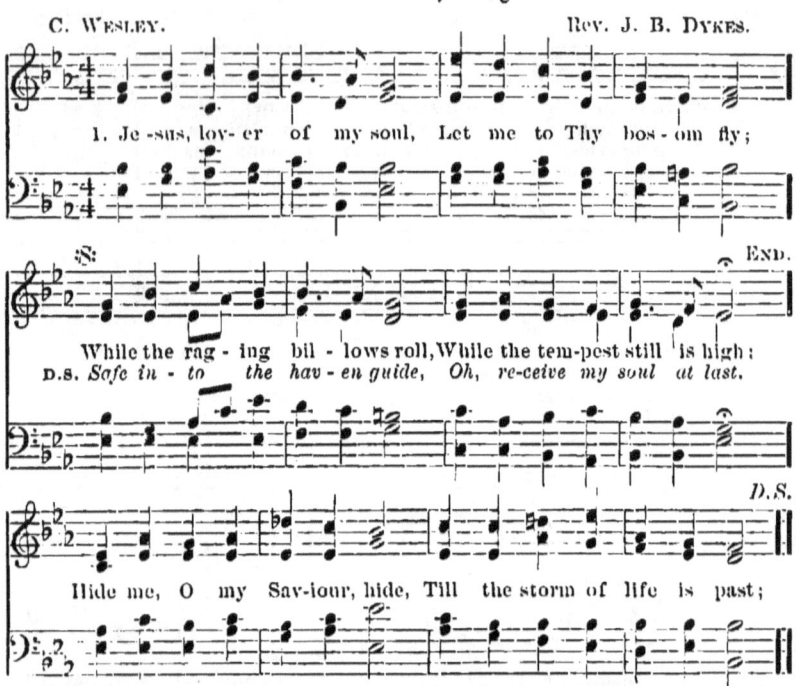

C. WESLEY. Rev. J. B. DYKES.

1. Je-sus, lov-er of my soul, Let me to Thy bos-om fly;
While the rag-ing bil-lows roll, While the tem-pest still is high:
D.S. Safe in-to the hav-en guide, Oh, re-ceive my soul at last.
Hide me, O my Sav-iour, hide, Till the storm of life is past;

2 Other refuge have I none;
  Hangs my helpless soul on Thee;
Leave, ah! leave me not alone,
  Still support and comfort me;
All my trust on Thee is stayed,
  All my help from Thee I bring;
Cover my defenceless head
  With the shadow of Thy wing.

3 Thou, O Christ! art all I want,
  All in all in Thee I find;
Raise the fallen, cheer the faint,
  Heal the sick and lead the blind;

Just and holy is Thy name,
  I am all unrighteousness:
Vile and full of sin I am,
  Thou art full of truth and grace.

4 Plenteous grace with Thee is found
  Grace to pardon all my sin;
Let the healing streams abound,
  Make and keep me pure within;
Thou, of life, the fountain art,
  Freely let me take of Thee;
Spring Thou up within my heart;
  Rise to all eternity.

182 Martyn.

S. B. MARSH.

183. Christ in the Vessel.

NEWTON. KARL REDEN. By per.

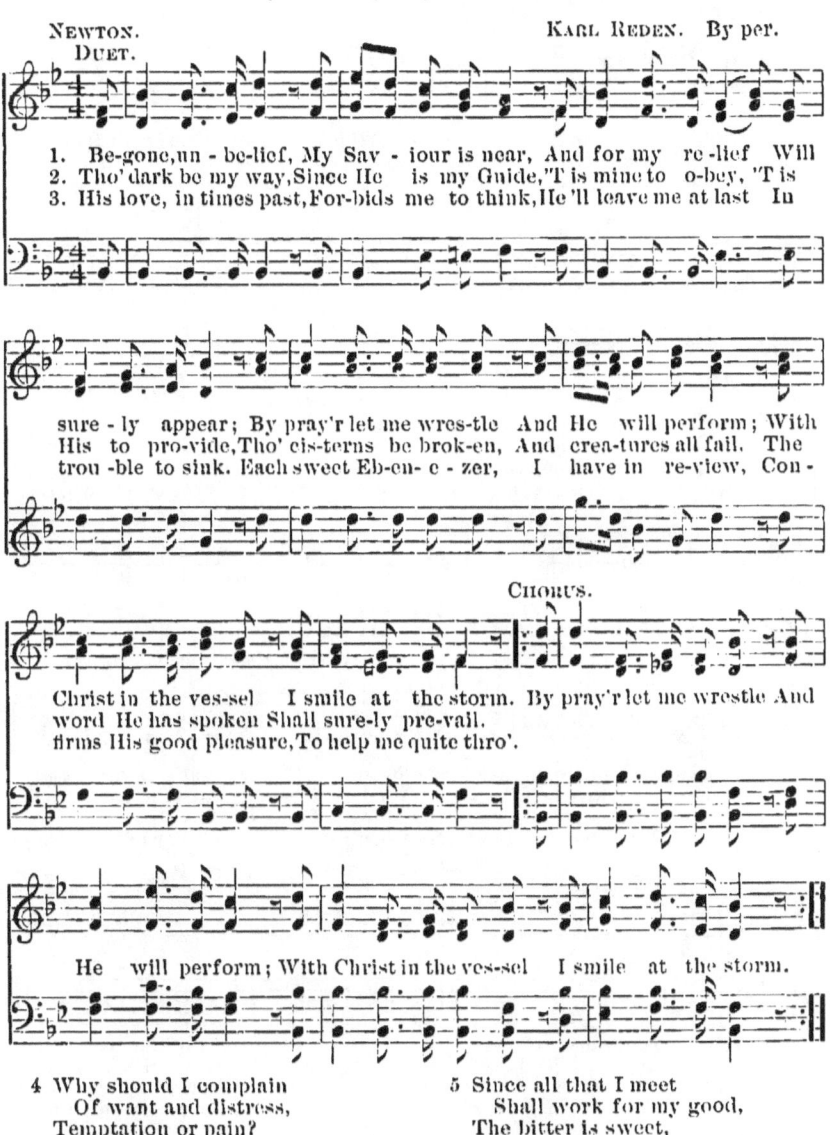

1. Be-gone, un-be-lief, My Saviour is near, And for my relief Will surely appear; By pray'r let me wrestle And He will perform; With Christ in the vessel I smile at the storm. By pray'r let me wrestle And He will perform; With Christ in the vessel I smile at the storm.
2. Tho' dark be my way, Since He is my Guide, 'T is mine to obey, 'T is His to provide, Tho' cisterns be broken, And creatures all fail, The word He has spoken Shall surely prevail.
3. His love, in times past, Forbids me to think, He'll leave me at last In trouble to sink. Each sweet Eben-e-zer, I have in review, Confirms His good pleasure, To help me quite thro'.

4 Why should I complain
Of want and distress,
Temptation or pain?
He told me no less.
The heirs of salvation,
I know from His word,
Through much tribulation
Must follow their Lord. CHO.

5 Since all that I meet
Shall work for my good,
The bitter is sweet,
The medicine food:
Though painful at present,
'T will cease before long,
And then, O how pleasant
The Conqueror's song! CHO.

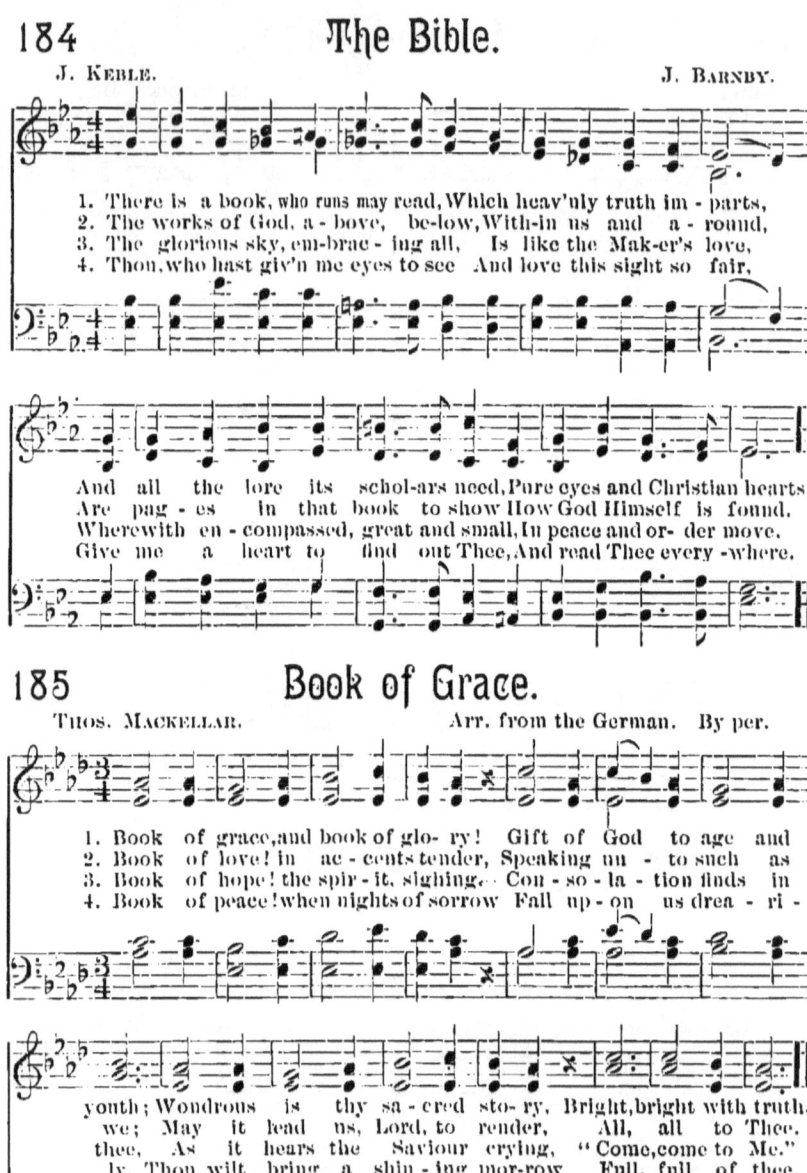

186. Just as I Am.

Arr. from the German. By per.

1. Just as I am, with-out one plea, But that Thy Blood was shed for me,
2. Just as I am, and wait-ing not To rid my soul of one dark blot,
3. Just as I am, tho' tossed about With many a conflict, many a doubt,
4. Just as I am, poor, wretched, blind,— Sight, riches, healing of the mind,

And that thou bid'st me come to thee, O Lamb of God, I come.
To Thee, whose blood can cleanse each spot, O Lamb of God, I come.
Fightings with-in, and fears with-out, O Lamb of God, I come.
Yea, all I need in Thee to find, O Lamb of God, I come.

5 Just as I am, Thou wilt receive,
Wilt welcome, pardon, cleanse, relieve;
Because Thy promise I believe;
O Lamb of God, I come.

6 Just as I am, for love unknown
Has broken ev'ry barrier down;
Now to be Thine, and Thine alone,
O Lamb of God, I come.

187. Just Now.

1. Come to Je-sus, Come to Je-sus, Come to Je-sus just now; Just now come to Je-sus, Come to Je-sus just now.

2 He will save you, He will save you,
   He will save you just now;
   Just now He will save you,
   He will save you just now.

3 He is able, etc.

4 He is willing, etc.

5 He'll forgive you, etc.

6 Don't reject Him, etc.

7 Only trust Him, etc.

8 Hallelujah, hallelujah,
  Hallelujah, Amen,
  Amen, hallelujah, etc.

188. My Days are gliding swiftly by.

Arr. from the German. By per.

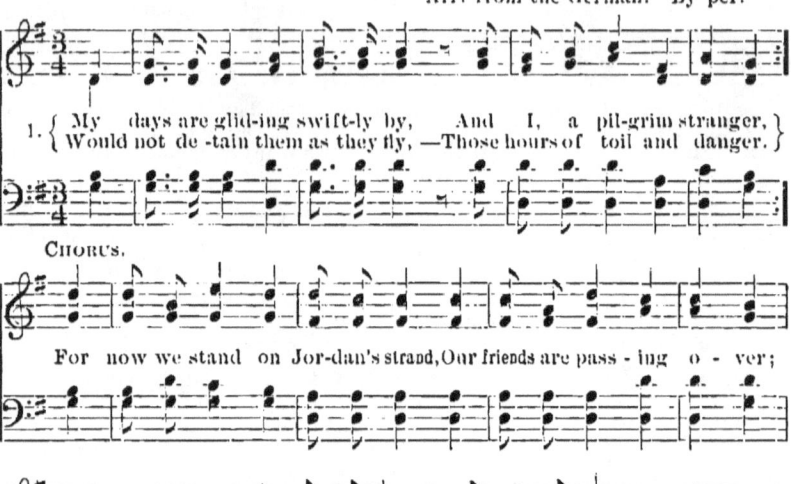

1. My days are glid-ing swift-ly by, And I, a pil-grim stranger,
Would not de-tain them as they fly, —Those hours of toil and danger.

CHORUS.
For now we stand on Jor-dan's strand, Our friends are pass-ing o-ver;
And, just be-fore, the shin-ing shore We may al-most dis-cov-er.

2 Our absent King the watchword gave,—
 "Let ev'ry lamp be burning;"
We look afar, across the wave,
 Our distant home discerning. CHO.

3 Should coming days be dark and cold,
 We will not yield to sorrow,

For hope will sing, with courage bold,
 "There's glory on the morrow." CHO.

4 Let storms of woe in whirlwinds rise,
 Each cord on earth to sever,—
There—bright and joyous in the skies,
 There—is our home forever. CHO.

189. Even Me.

Arr. from the German. By per.

1. Lord, I hear of show'rs of blessing Thou art scatt'ring full and free;
Show'rs the thirsty land re-freshing, Let some droppings fall on me,

EVEN ME.

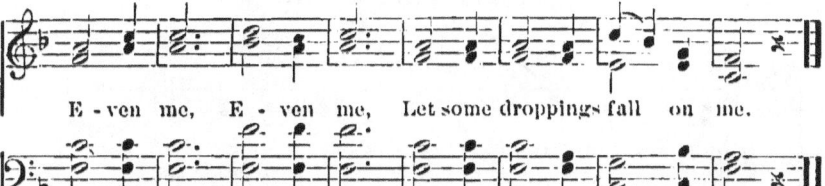

2. Pass me not, O God our Father!
Sinful though my heart may be;
Thou might'st leave me, but the rather
Let Thy mercy light on me,
Even me.

3. Pass me not, O gracious Saviour!
Let me live, and cling to Thee!
Oh! I'm longing for Thy favor —
While Thou'rt calling, oh, call me!
Even me.

4. Pass me not, O mighty Spirit!
Thou canst make the blind to see;
Witnesser of Jesus' merit,
Speak some word of power to me,
Even me.

5. Pass me not! Thy lost one bringing
Bind, oh, bind my heart to Thee;
While the streams of life are springing,
Blessing others—oh, bless me!
Even me.

190 Jesus, the very thought of Thee.

HAYDN.

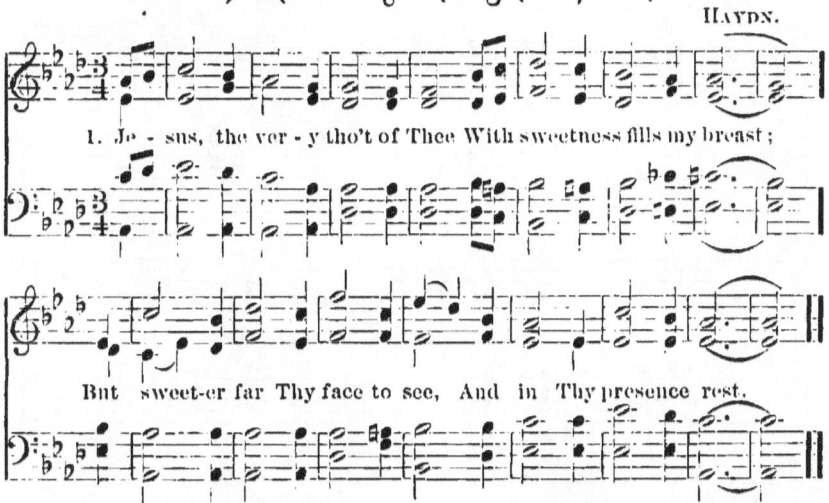

2. Nor voice can sing, nor heart can frame,
Nor can the mem'ry find
A sweeter sound than Thy blest name,
O Saviour of mankind!

3. O hope of ev'ry contrite heart,
O joy of all the meek,
To those who fall, how kind Thou art!
How good to those who seek!

4. But what to those who find? Ah, this,
Nor tongue nor pen can show:
The love of Jesus, what it is,
None but His loved ones know.

5. Jesus, our only joy be Thou,
As Thou our prize wilt be;
Jesus, be Thou our glory now,
And through eternity.

191. Jesus paid it all.

Miss Pease.

1. Nothing either great or small, Remains for me to do;
   Jesus died, and paid it all — Yes, all the debt I owe.

2. When He from His lofty throne Stoop'd down to do and die,
   Ev'ry-thing was fully done; "'T is finish'd!" was His cry.

CHORUS.
Jesus paid it all, All the debt I owe,
Jesus died and paid it all, Yes, all the debt I owe.

3 Weary, working, plodding one,
  Oh, wherefore toil you so?
  Cease your doing — all was done;
  Yes, ages long ago.

4 Till to Jesus' work you cling,
  Alone by simple faith,
  "Doing" is a deadly thing,
  Your "doing," ends in death.

5 Cast your deadly "doing" down,
  Down all at Jesus' feet;
  Stand in Him, in Him alone,
  All glorious and complete.

192. The Garden of Spices.

Mrs. Margaret J. Preston.   Arr. from the Scotch. By per.

DUET.

1. Let us go where the rose Of sweet Sharon is blowing, Let us search in the vale Where the lil-y is growing; Let us seek till we find In the garden of spi-ces, Our Beloved, Whose love Ev'ry longing suffices.

2. Let us come in the morn Of our youth and our gladness, Nor delay till our brows Wear the sere leaves of sadness. Let us bring Him our hearts Ere the world hath yet won them. For the buds are most sweet, While the dew is upon them.

3. Let us follow His steps; With our Saviour before us, With the light of His truth Shining steadily o'er us, We will learn that His love Ev'ry longing suffices, That communion with Him Is our garden of spices!

CHORUS.

Let us go where the rose And the lil-y are blowing, Where the waters of life In their freshness are flowing.

195. Ready. Chant.

Mrs. M. J. Preston.   Lesta Vese. By per.

1 I would be ready, | Lord,
   My | house in order | set,‖
  None of the work Thou | gavest me
   To do, un | finished | yet.

2 I would be watching, | Lord, [clear,‖
   With | lamp well-trimmed and |
  Quick to throw open | wide the door,
   What | time Thou drawest | near.

3 I would be waiting, | Lord,
   Be | cause I cannot | know‖

If in the night or | morning watch
   I | may be called to | go.

4 I would be working, | Lord,
   Each | day, each hour for | Thee,‖
  Assured that thus I | wait Thee well,
   When- | e'er Thy coming | be.

5 I would be living, | Lord,
   As | ever in Thine | eye ;‖
  For whoso lives the | holiest life
   Is readiest to | die.

196. Only Believe. Chant.

Mrs. M. J. Preston.   Lesta Vese. By per.

1 What is it to believe?
   To take Christ | at His | word ‖
  As if right out of Heaven,
   His | loving voice | I heard,—‖
    "Only believe."

2 What is it to believe?
   That God's Be | loved | Son ‖
  Has kept for me the laws
   I've | broken every | one ;‖
    "Only believe."

3 What is it to believe?
   To come to | Him and | say,‖
  "Against Thee have I sinned,—
   Take | Thou my sins a- | way."‖
    "Only believe."

4 What is it to believe?
   With eyes through | sorrow | dim,‖
  To take His seamless robe,
   And | leave my rags to | Him.‖
    "Only believe."

5 What is it to believe?
   To compre- | hend how | I ‖
  Escape through Him the curse,
   The | soul that sins, must | die.‖
    "Only believe."

6 What is it to believe?
   Upon His | cross di- | vine ‖
  To look and know that God
   Ac- | cepts His death for | mine.‖
    "Only believe."

7 What is it to believe?
   To love Him | for His | grace,‖
  Who comes, obeys and dies,
   All | in my room and | place.‖
    "Only believe."

8 This is that saving faith
   The sinner | must re- | ceive,—‖
  This is that life from death,
   This | is it to believe !‖
    "Only believe."

197. None, or All!

Mrs. Margaret J. Preston.   *Arr. from the German. By per.*

1. "Lord, I will follow Thee," I said, "And give to Thee my heart: And for the world and self will keep Only a little part;
A little part what time my soul Grows weary-worn and sad,— A little spot where earthly joys May come and make me glad."
But on my ear it seemed to me, I heard a whisper fall; "I cannot halve thy heart with thee, Give none to Me—or all!"

2 "But, Lord, the world is fair," I said,
"I would not go astray,
Yet may I sometimes pluck a flow'r
Outside the narrow way?
Yet may I sometimes sit serene,
Nor Spirit-conflicts share,
And for a little shift the cross
I am content to bear?"
Yet once again it seemed to me,
I heard the whisper fall:
"I cannot halve thy heart with thee,
Give none to Me,— or all!"

3 "Ah, Lord, my every hope," I said,
"On Thee alone I rest,
And I am sure the very way
Thou leadest me, is best: [path,
And if I've thought too straight my
Too stern my hind'ring vows,
Teach me that nought of real joy
Thy service disallows."
Again more soft, it seemed to me,
I heard the whisper fall: [thee,
"I will not halve My heav'n with
Then give to Me thine all!"

199. Because. Chant.

Mrs. Margaret J. Preston. Karl Reden. By per.

2 With restless passions surging like a sea,
How | can I think to find repose for | Thee? ‖
—Because Thy voice hushed stormy | Galli- | lee.

3 With guilt's defilement clothed without, within,
How | can I hope Thy pardoning grace to | win? ‖
—Because Thou saidst — "I have for- | given thy | sin."

4 With earth's poor, piteous toilings tired, opprest,
What | right have I to lean upon Thy | breast? ‖
—Because Thou offerest to the | weary, | rest.

5 With heart-affections stony-cold and dead,
What | claim have I to plead for life in- | stead? ‖
—Because in Joseph's tomb was | laid Thy | head!

200. Jerusalem the Golden.

From the English.

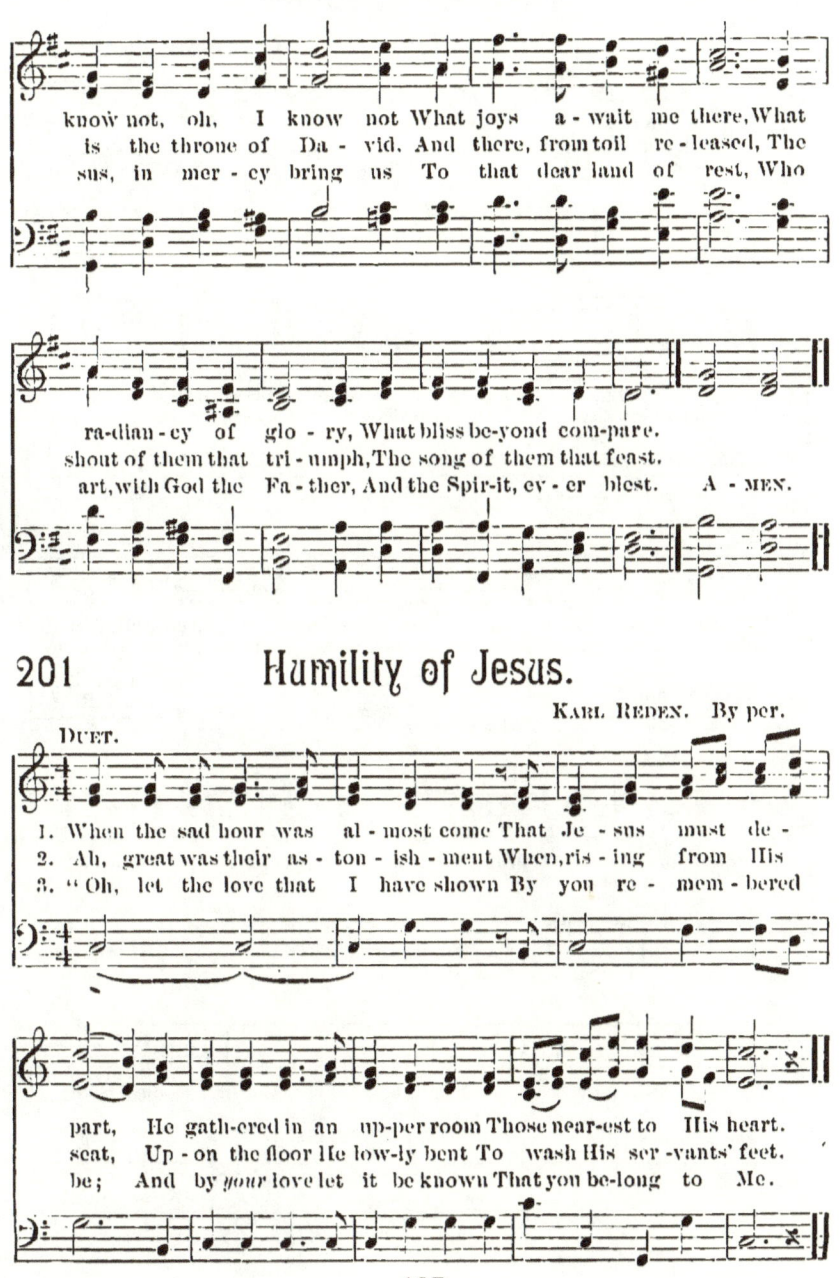

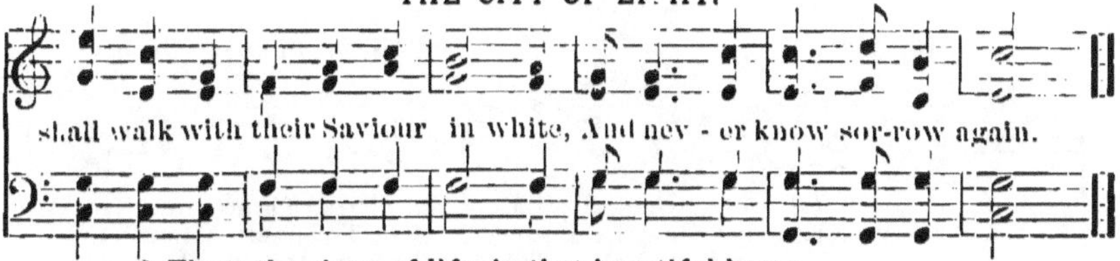

THE CITY OF LIGHT.

...shall walk with their Saviour in white, And nev-er know sor-row again.

3 There the river of life, in that beautiful home,
From the throne of our God ever flows,
And the great trees of life, by that river so clear,
Their twelve manner of fruit for the glorified bear,
Who by its still waters repose. Cho.

4 Oh, what glittering crowns, in that beautiful home,
The ransomed forever shall wear,
While with harps in their hands, they forever shall sing
Sweetest anthems of praise to their Saviour and King,
For no sickness, nor death enters there. Cho.

203 Mission Hymn.

J. MARRIOTT.   J. B. DYKES.

1. Thou, whose al-might-y word Cha- os and dark-ness heard,
2. Thou, who didst come to bring On Thy re-deem-ing wing
3. Spir-it of truth and love, Life-giv-ing, ho-ly Dove,
4. Bless-ed and ho-ly Three, Glo-ri-ous Trin-i-ty,

And took their flight; Hear us, we hum-bly pray, And where the
Heal-ing and sight, Health to the sick in mind, Sight to the
Speed forth Thy flight; Move o'er the wa-ter's face, Bear-ing the
Wis-dom, Love, Might: Bound-less as o-cean's tide, Roll-ing in

gos-pel's day Sheds not its glo-rious ray, "Let there be light."
in-ly blind, O, now to all man-kind "Let there be light."
lamp of grace, And in earth's dark-est place "Let there be light."
full-est pride, Thro' the world, far and wide, "Let there be light."

ONE SWEETLY SOLEMN THOUGHT.

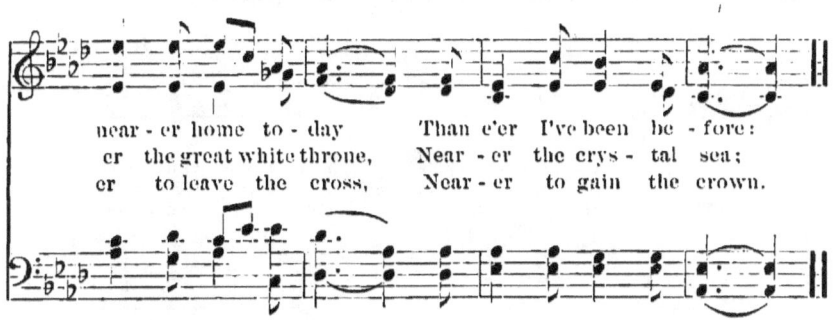

near-er home to-day   Than e'er I've been be-fore:
er the great white throne,   Near-er the crys-tal sea;
er to leave the cross,   Near-er to gain the crown.

4 The waves of that deep sea
　Roll dark before my sight,
　But break, the other side,
　Upon a shore of light.

5 Oh! if my mortal feet
　Have almost gained the brink,

If I am nearer home
To-day than e'en I think:

6 Father! perfect my trust,
　That I may rest in death,
　On Christ, my Lord, alone,
　And thus resign my breath.

206 St. Hugh.

H. F. LYTE.　　　　　　　　　　　E. J. HOPKINS.
S. S. SOLO.

1. O Lord, how good, how great art Thou, In heav'n and earth the same;
2. When glo-rious in the night-ly sky Thy moon and stars I see,
3. Close to Thine own bright ser-a-phim His fav-ored path is trod;

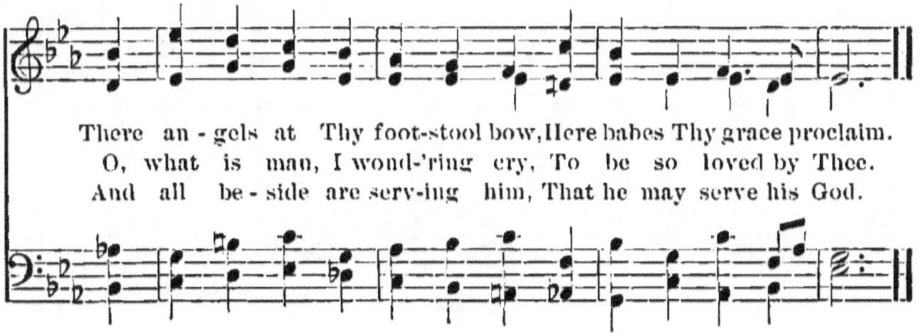

There an-gels at Thy foot-stool bow, Here babes Thy grace proclaim.
O, what is man, I wond'ring cry, To be so loved by Thee.
And all be-side are serv-ing him, That he may serve his God.

209. Gethsemane.

J. MONTGOMERY.   R. REDHEAD.

1. Go to dark Geth-se-ma-ne, Ye that feel the tempter's pow'r;
2. Fol-low to the judgment-hall, View the Lord of life arraigned;
3. Calv'ry's mournful mountain climb; There, ador-ing at His feet,
4. Ear-ly has-ten to the tomb, Where they laid His breathless clay:

Your Re-deem-er's con-flict see, Watch with Him one bit-ter hour:
O the wormwood and the gall! O the pangs His soul sus-tained!
Mark that mir-a-cle of time, God's own sac-ri-fice complete:
All is sol-i-tude and gloom; Who hath tak-en Him a-way?

Turn not from His griefs a-way, Learn of Je-sus Christ to pray.
Shun not suffering, shame or loss; Learn of Him to bear the cross.
"It is fin-ished," hear the cry; Learn of Je-sus Christ to die.
Christ is risen; He meets our eyes; Sav-iour, teach us so to rise.

210. Who Givest All.

C. WORDSWORTH.   J. B. DYKES.

1. O Lord of heaven and earth and sea, To Thee all praise and

WHO GIVEST ALL.

glo - ry be: How shall we show our love to Thee Who givest all?

2 The golden sunshine, vernal air,
Sweet flow'rs and fruit Thy love de-
clare:
When harvests ripen, Thou art there,
Who givest all.

3 For peaceful homes, and healthful
days,
For all the blessings earth displays,
We owe thee thankfulness and praise,
Who givest all.

4 For souls redeemed, for sins forgiv'n,
For means of grace and hopes of
heav'n;

What can to Thee, O Lord, be giv'n,
Who givest all?

5 We lose what on ourselves we spend;
We have as treasure without end
Whatever, Lord, to Thee we lend,
Who givest all.

6 Whatever, Lord, we lend to Thee,
Repaid a thousandfold will be;
Then gladly will we give to Thee,
Who givest all.

211 Morning Hymn.

C. C. CONVERSE. By per.

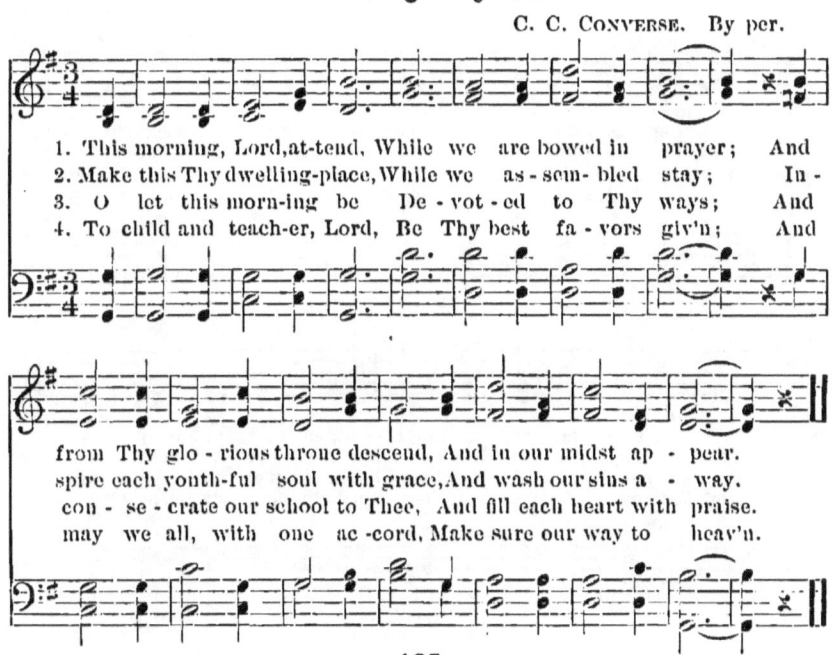

1. This morning, Lord, at-tend, While we are bowed in prayer; And from Thy glo - rious throne descend, And in our midst ap - pear.
2. Make this Thy dwelling-place, While we as - sem - bled stay; In - spire each youth-ful soul with grace, And wash our sins a - way.
3. O let this morn-ing be De - vot - ed to Thy ways; And con - se - crate our school to Thee, And fill each heart with praise.
4. To child and teach-er, Lord, Be Thy best fa - vors giv'n; And may we all, with one ac -cord, Make sure our way to heav'n.

213. The Story of the Cross.

E. Monro.   A. Redhead.

1. In His own raiment clad, With His blood dyed; Wo-men walk sorrow-ing By His side.
2. O, whither wandering Bear they that tree? He Who first carries it, Who is He?
3. Follow to Cal-va-ry, Tread where He trod, He Who for ever was Son of God.
4. Is there no beauty to You who pass by In that lone figure which Marks the sky?

5. On the cross lifted up, Thy face we scan, Bearing that cross for us, Son of man.
6. Thorns form Thy diadem, Rough wood Thy throne; For us Thy blood is shed, Us a-lone.
7. No pillow under Thee To rest Thy head, On-ly the splintered cross Is Thy bed.
8. What, O my Saviour! Here didst Thou see, Which made Thee suffer and Die for me?

9. O I will follow Thee, Star of my soul, Thro' the deep shades of life To the goal.
11. Lord, if Thou on-ly wilt Make me Thine own, Give no com-panion, save Thee a-lone.

10. Yes, let Thy cross be borne Each day by me, Mind not how heavy if But with Thee.
12. Grant thro' each day of life To stand by Thee; With Thee, when morning breaks, Ever to be.

214. The Cross.

ISSAC WATTS. GOUNOD.

1. When I sur-vey the wondrous cross, On which the Prince of glo-ry died,
2. For-bid it, Lord! that I should boast, Save in the death of Christ, my God;
3. See! from His head, His hands, His feet, Sorrow and love flow mingled down;

My rich-est gain I count but loss, And pour con-tempt on all my pride.
All the vain things that charm me most, I sac-ri-fice them to His blood.
Did e'er such love and sorrow meet? Or thorns compose so rich a crown?

REFRAIN.

The cross! The cross! The won-drous cross On which the Prince of glo-ry died.

4 His dying crimson, like a robe,
  Spreads o'er His body on the tree;
Then am I dead to all the globe,
  And all the globe is dead to me.
    REF.

5 Were the whole realm of nature mine,
  That were a present far too small;
Love so amazing, so divine,
  Demands my soul, my life, my all.
    REF.

215. Children's Prayer.

W. H. Groser.   E. C. Revons. By per.

1. Sav-iour, Lord, we bow be-fore Thee, On this day of ju-bi-lee; And with hum-ble hearts implore Thee, That a-mong us Thou wilt be. Thou wilt be, Thou wilt be, That among us Thou wilt be.

2. God of love! what thanks we owe Thee For the gos-pel of Thy grace! May we all be taught to know Thee, Ear-ly led to seek Thy face. Seek Thy face, Seek Thy face, Ear-ly led to seek Thy face.

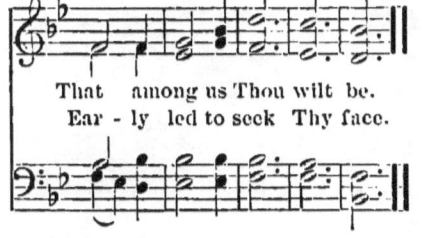

3 Now, for every gift and blessing,
   We would render grateful praise;
  And to Thee, our sins confessing,
   Dedicate our future days.

4 If our hearts to Thee be given,
   We Thy face at length shall see;
  And around Thy throne in heaven
   Spend an endless jubilee.

217. All for Jesus.

Mary D. James. — Adapted. By per.

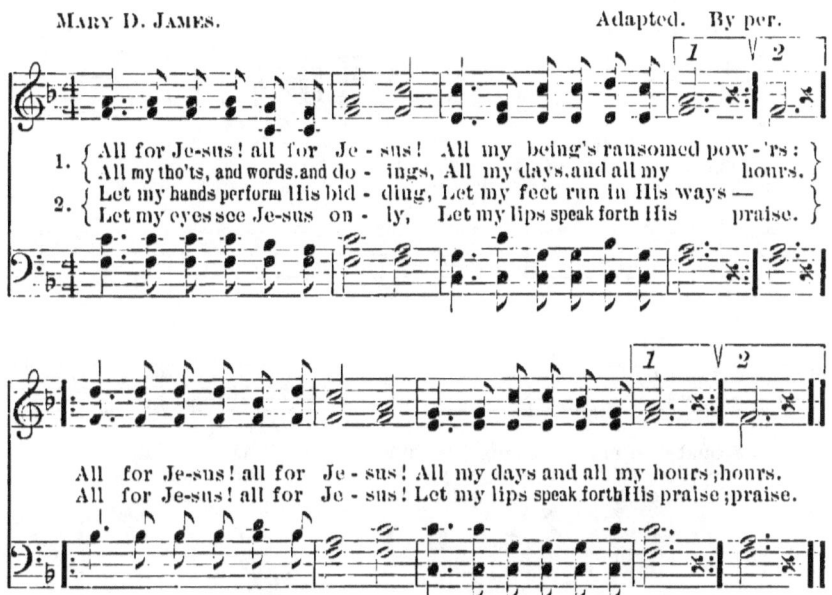

1. All for Jesus! all for Jesus! All my being's ransomed pow-'rs:
   All my tho'ts, and words, and do - ings, All my days, and all my hours.
2. Let my hands perform His bid - ding, Let my feet run in His ways —
   Let my eyes see Jesus on - ly, Let my lips speak forth His praise.

All for Jesus! all for Jesus! All my days and all my hours; hours.
All for Jesus! all for Jesus! Let my lips speak forth His praise; praise.

3 Since my eyes were fixed on Jesus,
   I've lost sight of all besides;
   So enchained my spirit's vision,
   Looking at the Crucified.
   ‖: All for Jesus! all for Jesus!
   Looking at the Crucified. :‖

4 Oh, what wonder! how amazing!
   Jesus, glorious King of kings —
   Deigns to call me His beloved,
   Lets me rest beneath His wings.
   ‖: All for Jesus! all for Jesus!
   Resting now beneath His wings! :‖

218. Remember Me.

Karl Reden. By per.

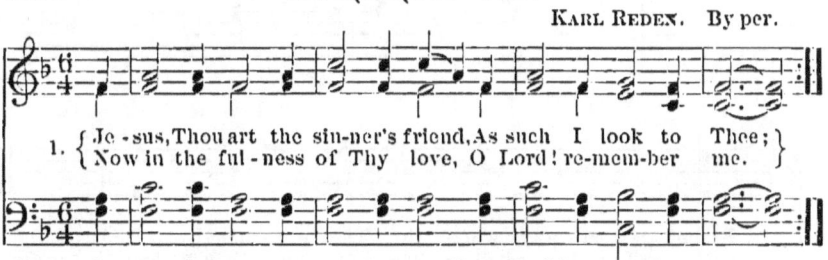

1. Je - sus, Thou art the sin-ner's friend, As such I look to Thee;
   Now in the ful - ness of Thy love, O Lord! re-mem-ber me.

Cho.— Re - mem-ber me, re - mem-ber me, Dear Lord! re - mem-ber me.

2 Remember Thy pure word of grace,
   Remember Calvary;
   Remember all Thy dying groans,
   And then remember me. Cho.

3 Lord! I am guilty — I am vile,
   But Thy salvation's free;
   Then, in Thine all-abounding grace,
   Dear Lord! remember me. Cho.

220. The Soul's Anchor.

Arr. from WALLACE. By per.

1. Now I have found the ground wherein, Sure my soul's anchor may re-main; The wounds of Je-sus for my sin, Be-fore the world's sal-va-tion slain. His mer-cy shall unshaken stay, When heav'n and earth are fled away, His mercy shall un-shak-en stay, When heav'n and earth are fled away, When heav'n and earth are fled away.

2 O Lord, Thine everlasting grace
   Our scanty thought surpasses far:
   Thy heart still melts with tenderness;
   Thine arms of love still open are,
   Returning sinners to receive,
   That mercy they may taste, and live.

3 O love, thou bottomless abyss!
   My sins are swallowed up in thee;
   All cover'd my unrighteousness,
   Nor spot of guilt remains on me:
   While Jesus' blood, thro' earth and skies
   His mercy, boundless mercy, cries.

4 By faith, I plunge me in this sea;
   Here is my hope, my joy, my rest;
   Hither, when hell assails, I flee;
   I look into my Saviour's breast:
   Away, sad doubt and anxious fear!
   His mercy's all that's written there.

221. Hear Thy Children.

C. S. SMITH.   C. C. CONVERSE. By per.

1. Hear Thy chil-dren, gen-tle Je-sus, While we breathe our ev-'ning pray'r;
2. Gen-tle Je-sus! look in pit-y From Thy glo-rious throne a-bove;

Save us from all harm and dan-ger, Take us 'neath Thy shelt'ring care.
Tho' we sleep, Thy heart is wakeful, Still for us it beats with love.

Shield us from the wiles of Sa-tan, From the per-ils of this night;
Shades of ev-'ning fast are fall-ing, Day is fad-ing in-to gloom;

Safe-ly may Thy guar-dian an-gels Keep us in their watchful sight.
When our earth-ly life is end-ed, Lead Thy ran-som'd children home.

223 This is the Day of Toil.

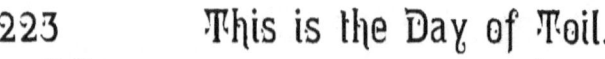

H. BONAR. LESTA VESE. By per.

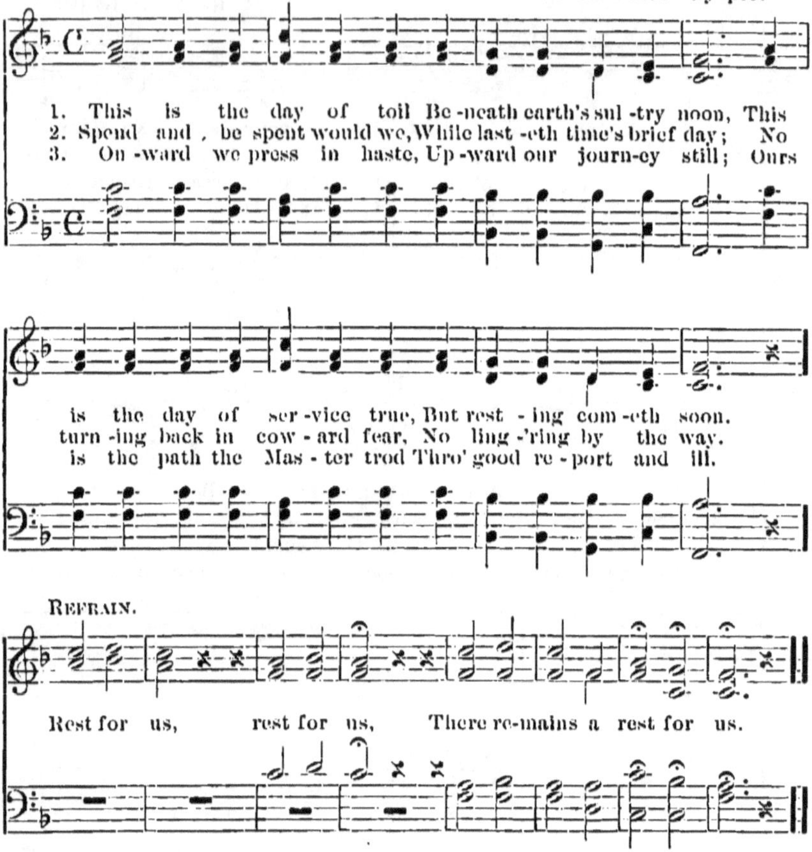

1. This is the day of toil Be-neath earth's sul-try noon, This
2. Spend and, be spent would we, While last-eth time's brief day; No
3. On-ward we press in haste, Up-ward our journ-ey still; Ours
is the day of ser-vice true, But rest-ing com-eth soon.
turn-ing back in cow-ard fear, No ling-'ring by the way.
is the path the Mas-ter trod Thro' good re-port and ill.
REFRAIN.
Rest for us, rest for us, There re-mains a rest for us.

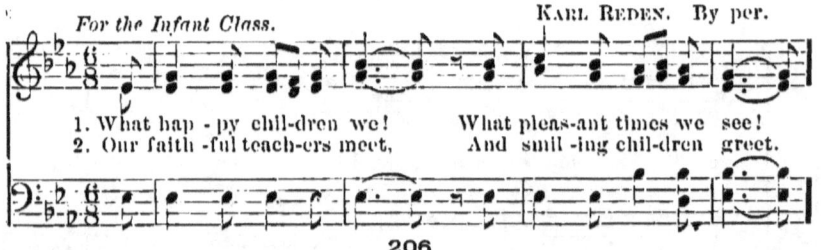

224 Happy Children.

For the Infant Class. KARL REDEN. By per.

1. What hap-py chil-dren we! What pleas-ant times we see!
2. Our faith-ful teach-ers meet, And smil-ing chil-dren greet.

HAPPY CHILDREN.

In the Sunday-school, the Sunday-school, What happy children we?

225 I Bring my Sins to Thee.

F. R. HAVERGAL. C. C. CONVERSE. By per.

1. I bring my sins to Thee, The sins I can-not count, That all may cleans-ed be, In the once o-pen'd Fount: I bring them, Sav-iour, all to Thee; The bur-den is too great for me.
2. I bring my grief to Thee, The grief I can-not tell; No words shall need-ed be, Thou know-est all so well: I bring the sor-row laid on me, O suf-f'ring Sav-iour! all to Thee.
3. My joys to Thee I bring, The joys Thy love has giv'n, That each may be a wing To lift me near-er heav'n: I bring them, Sav-iour, all to Thee, Who hast pro-cured them all for me.
4. My life I bring to Thee, I would not be my own; O Sav-iour, let me be Thine, ev-er Thine a-lone. My heart, my life, my all, I bring To Thee, my Sav-iour and my King.

226. Jesus and His Cross.

LESTA VESE. By per.

1. Of Jesus and His cross I sing; My best affections cluster there; Thence all my sweetest comforts spring, Joys to my soul, than life more dear.

2. I love to linger near the cross, And feel as if my God was there; It makes me count the world but dross, And fills my soul with faith and pray'r.

DUET.

Jesus and His cross I sing, Jesus and His cross I sing, His cross I sing.

D.C.

3 While with a melting heart I gaze,
　And drink my Saviour's sorrows in,
He bows His head, and sweetly says,
　"'Tis finished; there's an end of sin."

4 Strangely my sorrows turn to joy,
　I hail the dying, conqu'ring King;
The victor's crowns my tho'ts employ,
　And Christ, the living Christ, I sing.

227 How can we sing the Praise of Jesus?

3. How can we ever slight our Saviour?
Daily offend our gracious Lord?
All that we do for love of Jesus,
Surely brings us a rich reward!
Chorus for 3d verse.
Let us then have a heart to labor;
Consecrating ourselves anew;
Let us show our love for the blessed Saviour,
In whatsoever we may find to do.

228. In the Cross.

C. C. Converse. By per.

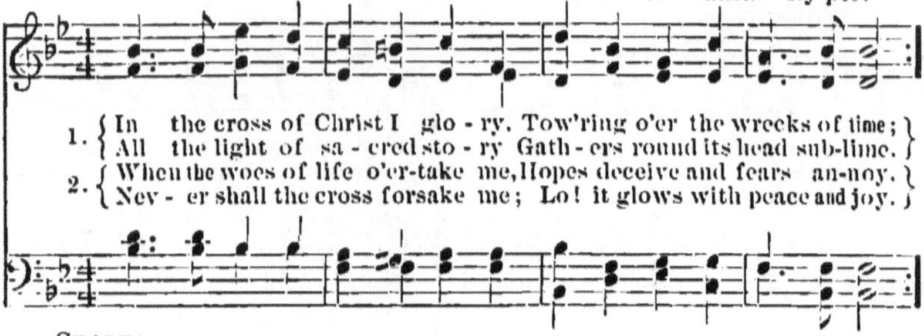

1. In the cross of Christ I glo-ry, Tow'ring o'er the wrecks of time;
   All the light of sa-cred sto-ry Gath-ers round its head sub-lime.
2. When the woes of life o'er-take me, Hopes deceive and fears an-noy,
   Nev-er shall the cross forsake me; Lo! it glows with peace and joy.

Chorus.

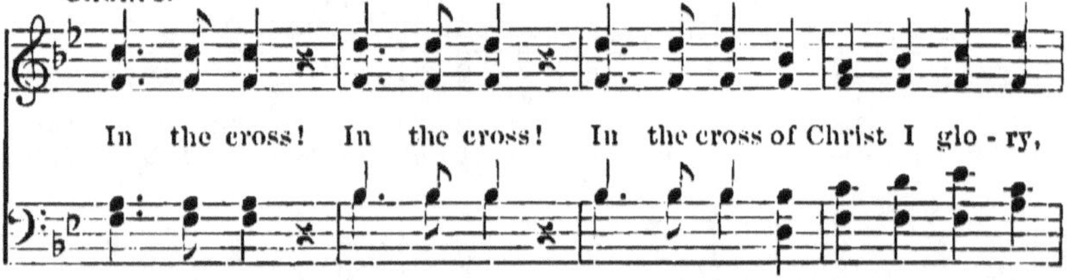

In the cross! In the cross! In the cross of Christ I glo-ry,
In the cross! In the cross! I glo-ry, in the cross.

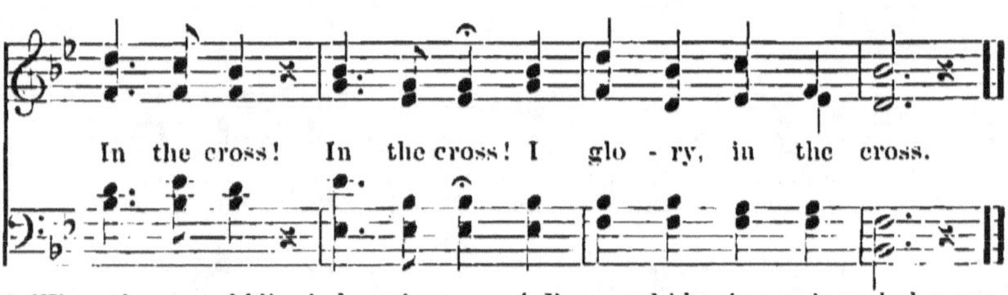

3 When the sun of bliss is beaming,
  Light and love upon my way,
  From the cross the radiance streaming
  Adds more lustre to the day. Cho.

4 Bane and blessing, pain and pleasure,
  By the cross are sanctified;
  Peace is there that knows no measure,
  Joy that thro' all time abides. Cho.

229. The youngest may come.

A. Arnott.　　　　　　　　　　Lesta Vese. By per.

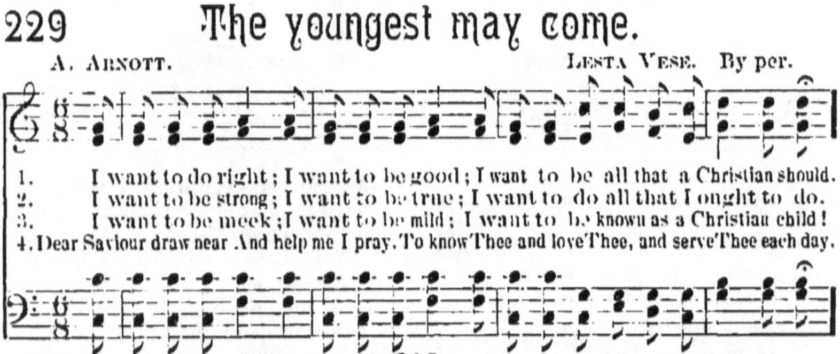

1. I want to do right; I want to be good; I want to be all that a Christian should.
2. I want to be strong; I want to be true; I want to do all that I ought to do.
3. I want to be meek; I want to be mild; I want to be known as a Christian child!
4. Dear Saviour draw near, And help me I pray, To know Thee and love Thee, and serve Thee each day.

THE YOUNGEST MAY COME.

For I'm nev-er too young, Nev-er too small to serve my dear Redeemer.

230 Glory be to God the Father

H. BONAR.   C. C. CONVERSE. By per.

1. Glo-ry be to God the Fa-ther, Glo-ry be to God the Son.
Glo-ry be to God the Spir-it, Great Je-ho-vah, Three in One:
Glo-ry, glo-ry, glo-ry, glo-ry, Glo-ry while e-ter-nal a-ges roll.

2 Glory be to Him who loved us,
   Washed us from each spot and stain;
Glory be to Him who bought us,
   Made us kings with Him to reign:
Glory, glory, glory, glory,
   Glory to the Lamb that once was slain!

3 Glory to the King of angels,
   Glory to the Church's King,
Glory to the King of nations,
   Heav'n and earth, your praises bring:
Glory, glory, glory, glory,
   Glory to the King of glory bring!

4 Glory, blessing, praise eternal!
   Thus the choir of angels sings;
Honor, riches, power, dominion!
   Thus its praise creation brings:
Glory, glory, glory, glory,
   Glory, glory to the King of kings!

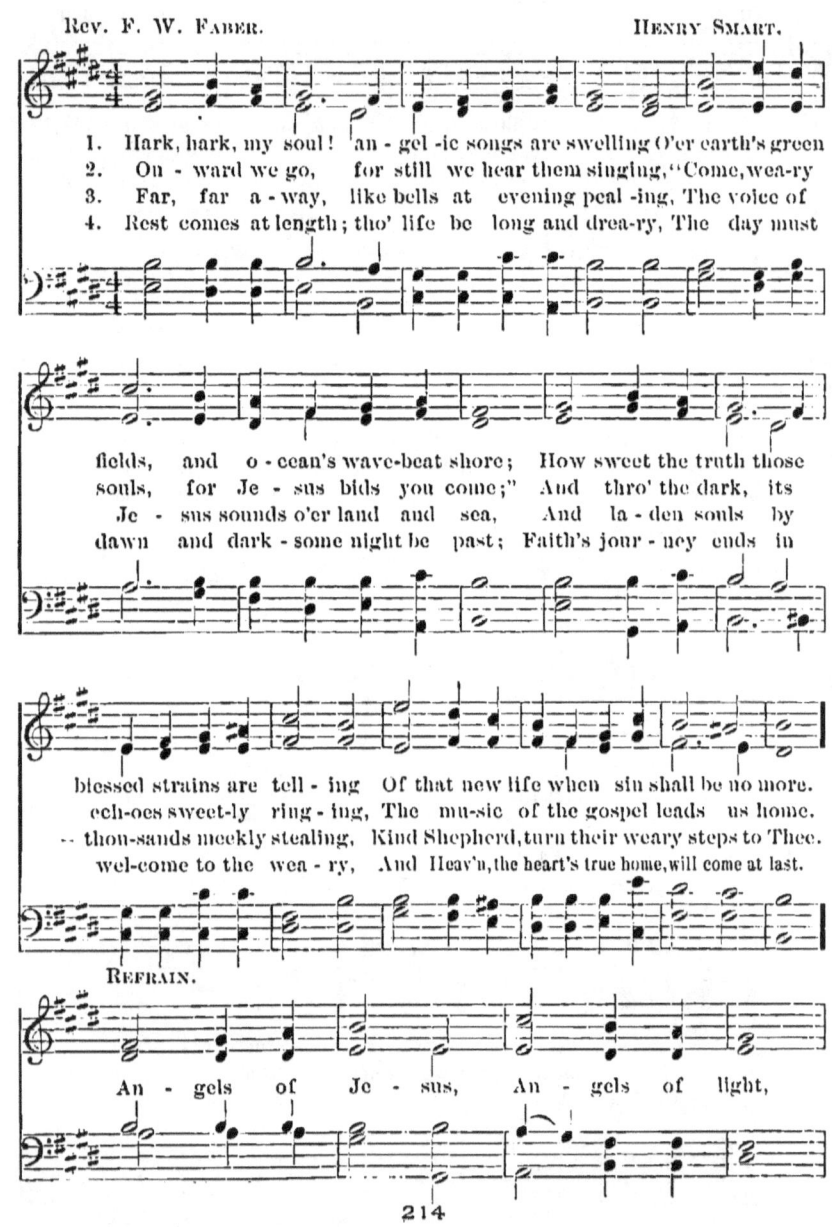

ON, ON MY SOUL.

Sing-ing to wel-come the pil-grims of the night.

5 Angels! sing on, your faithful watches keeping,
Sing us sweet fragments of the songs above;
Till morning's joy shall end the night of weeping,
And life's long shadows break in cloudless love.

234 To Thee, my God and Saviour!

T. HAWEIS. THALBERG.

To Thee, my God and Sav-iour! My heart ex-ult-ing sings,
Re-joic-ing in Thy fa-vor,
Almight-y King of kings! I'll cel-e-brate Thy glo-ry,
And tell the joy-ful sto-ry
With all Thy saints a-bove, Of Thy re-deem-ing love.

2 Soon as the morn, with roses,
    Bedecks the dewy east,
And when the sun reposes
    Upon the ocean's breast;
My voice, in supplication,
    Well-pleased Thou shalt hear;
Oh! grant me Thy salvation,
    And to my soul draw near.

3 By Thee, through life supported,
    I passed the dangerous road,
With heav'nly hosts escorted,
    Up to their bright abode;
There, cast my crown before Thee,—
    Now, all my conflicts o'er,—
And day and night adore Thee;—
    What can an angel more?

235. Early Seek, and You Shall Find.

Arr. from the German. By per.

1. Chil-dren! list-en to the Lord, And o-bey His gra-cious word;
2. Sor-row-ful your sins con-fess; Plead His per-fect right-eous-ness;
3. For His wor-ship now pre-pare; Kneel to Him in fer-vent prayer;

Seek His face with heart and mind; Ear-ly seek, and you shall find.
See the Sav-iour's bleeding side; Come! you will not be de-nied.
Serve Him with a per-fect heart; Nev-er from His ways de-part.

CHORUS.

Seek His face with heart and mind; Ear-ly seek, and you shall find.
See the Sav-iour's bleed-ing side; Come! you will not be de-nied.
Serve Him with a per-fect heart; Nev-er from His ways de-part.

Seek His face with heart and mind; Ear-ly seek, and you shall find.
See the Saviour's bleeding side; Come! you will not be de-nied.
Serve Him with a per-fect heart; Nev-er from His ways de-part.

236. God Speed the Right.

KARL REDEN. By per.

1. Brothers, sing with voice united, "God speed the right!" Sisters, join with hearts delighted, "God speed the right!" Lo! the winds in silence bearing, Lo! all nature's voice proclaiming, "God speed the right! God speed the right!"
2. Be ye firm and be enduring, "God speed the right!" Always in the right pursuing, "God speed the right!" When all obstacles impede thee, Trust in heav'n for strength to aid thee: "God speed the right! God speed the right!"
3. When life's conflicts all are over, "God speed the right!" May we ne'er prove faithless, never, "God speed the right!" When all earthly ties are sundered, When our days on earth are numbered, "God speed the right! God speed the right!"

237. To the Wandering.

KARL REDEN. By per.

1. To the wand'ring and the wea-ry, Ev-'rywhere, on land or sea,
Je-sus calls in tones of mer-cy, Je-sus calls in tones of mer-cy,
"Come un-to Me, Come, come un-to Me."

2 From our home, our household altar,
  Where our father bends the knee,
Oft we hear a voice inviting,
  "Come unto Me."

3 When, at night, upon our pillow,
  We have prayed our prayer to Thee,
Then we feel the word unspoken,
  "Come unto Me."

4 Oft we hear it when our teachers
  Talk to us of Calvary;
In our hearts the call re-echoes,
  "Come unto Me."

5 When we pass death's troubled river,
  Calm and peaceful it will be
If we hear our Saviour calling,
  "Come unto Me."

238. The Heavenly Sabbath.

KARL REDEN. By per.

1. Soon will set the Sab-bath sun, Soon the sa-cred day be gone;

THE HEAVENLY SABBATH.

2 Pleasant is the Sabbath bell,
  Seeming much of joy to tell;
  Kind our teachers are to-day,
  In the school we love to stay.

3 But a music, sweeter far,
  Breathes where angel-spirits are;
  Higher far than earthly strains,
  Where the rest of God remains.

4 Shall we ever rise to dwell
  Where immortal praises swell?
  And can children ever go
  Where eternal Sabbaths glow?

5 Yes:—that rest our own may be;
  All the good shall Jesus see;
  For the good a rest remains
  Where the glorious Saviour reigns.

239 Jesus, Hear and Save.

Adapted. By per.

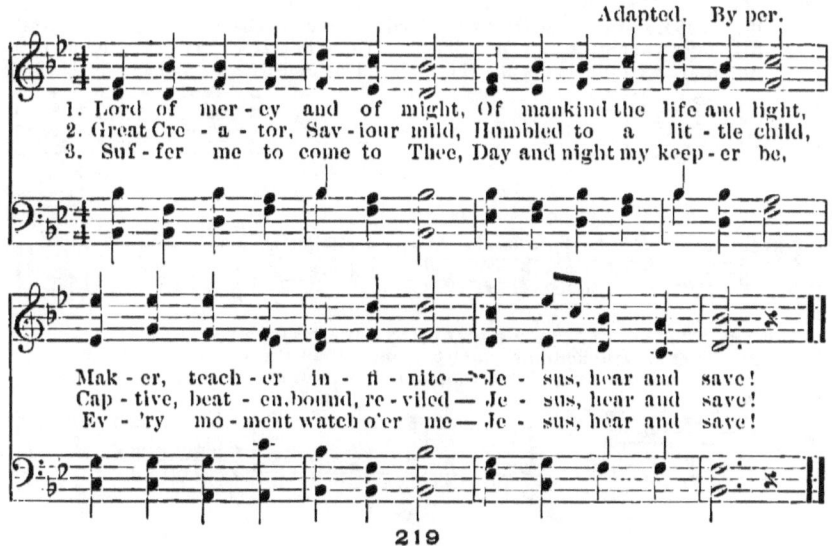

1. Lord of mer-cy and of might, Of mankind the life and light,
   Mak-er, teach-er in - fi - nite—Je-sus, hear and save!
2. Great Cre - a - tor, Sav-iour mild, Humbled to a lit-tle child,
   Cap-tive, beat - en, bound, re-viled— Je-sus, hear and save!
3. Suf-fer me to come to Thee, Day and night my keep-er be,
   Ev - 'ry mo-ment watch o'er me—Je-sus, hear and save!

2 If babes so many years ago
   His tender pity drew,
   He surely will not let me go
   Without a blessing too. Cho.

3 Then, while this favor to implore
   My little hands are spread;
   Do Thou Thy sacred blessing pour,
   Dear Jesus, on my head. Cho.

THE CHILDREN'S FRIEND.

To Thee we'll tune our songs of praise, To Thee, the Chil-dren's Friend; To Thee we'll tune our songs of praise, To Thee, the Chil-dren's Friend.
Oh, save our souls from sin and woe— Thou art the Chil-dren's Friend; Oh, save our souls from sin and woe— Thou art the Chil-dren's Friend.
Thus shall we learn to fear the Lord, And love the Chil-dren's Friend; Thus shall we learn to fear the Lord, And love the Chil-dren's Friend.

4 Oh, may we feel a Saviour's love,
   To Him our souls commend;
Who left His glorious throne above
   To be the Children's Friend.

5 Lord, draw our youthful hearts to Thee,
   And when this life shall end,
Raise us to live above the sky,
   With Thee, the Children's Friend.

244   The Little Children See.

Adapted. By per.

1. O gra-cious Lord of all, Thy lit-tle chil-dren see, And mer-ci-ful-ly call, Our wan-d'ring hearts to Thee.
2. O let Thy pow'r-ful grace Our souls' at-ten-tion draw, And on our mem-'ries trace Thy nev-er-chang-ing law.
3. Let faith, and hope, and love, To dwell in us u-nite, Then raise our souls a-bove, To live in end-less light.

248 Sweet as a Shepherd's Tuneful Reed.

W. SHIRLEY.   C. C. CONVERSE. By per.

1. Sweet as a Shep-herd's tune-ful reed, From Zi-on's mount I heard a sound; Gay sprang the flow'rets of the mead, And gladden'd nature smil'd a-round, The voice of peace salutes mine ear; Christ's lovely voice perfumes the air.

2. "Peace, troubled soul! whose plaintive moan Hath taught these rocks the note of woe; Cease thy complaint, suppress thy groan, And let thy tears forget to flow; Behold! the precious balm is found, Which lulls thy pain which heals thy wound.

3 Come, freely come, by sin oppressed
  Unburden here the weighty load;
Here find thy refuge and thy rest,
  Safe on the bosom of thy God:
Thy God's thy Saviour,— glorious word!
That sheaths th'avengers glitt'ring sword.

4 As spring, the winter,—day, the night,—
  Peace, sorrow's gloom shall chase away;
And smiling joy, a seraph bright,
  Shall tend thy steps and near thee stay;
Whilst glory weaves th'immortal crown,
And waits to claim thee for her own."

250. Threefold Love.

Tr. by R. Massie.   C. C. Converse.

1. See, Oh! see, what love the Fa-ther Hath be-stow'd up-on our race!
2. See, Oh! see, what love the Sav-iour, Al-so, hath on us be-stow'd!
3. See, Oh! see, what love is shown us, Al-so, by the Ho-ly Ghost!

How He bends, with sweet compas-sion, Ov-er us His beam-ing face!
How He bled for us and suf-fer'd, How He bore the heav-y load!
How He strives with us poor sin-ners, Ev-en when we sin the most,

See how He His best and dear-est, For the ver-y worst hath giv'n,—
On the cross and in the gar-den, Oh! how sore was His dis-tress!
Teaching, com-fort-ing, cor-rect-ing, Where He sees it need-ful is!

His own Son for us poor sin-ners; See, Oh! see the love of heav'n!
Is not this a love, that pass-eth Aught that tongue can e'er ex-press?
Oh! what heart would not be thank-ful For a threefold love like this?

WHEN FRIEND FROM FRIEND IS PARTING.

Thou wilt soothe us when we weep, And hear us when we pray.
Thou wilt soothe *them* when they weep, And hear *us* when we pray.
soothe us, Lord, oft as we weep, And hear us when we pray.

252. Children's Praise.

E. C. REVONS. By per.

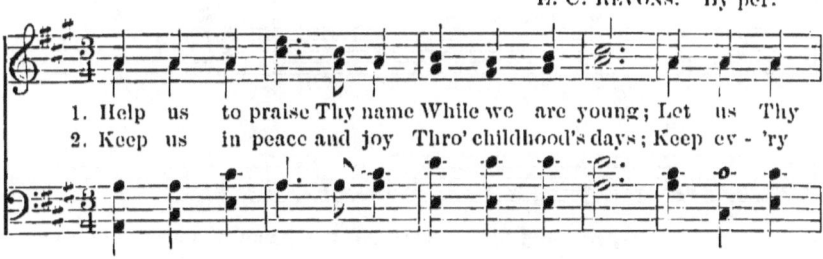

1. Help us to praise Thy name While we are young; Let us Thy
2. Keep us in peace and joy Thro' childhood's days; Keep ev - 'ry

END. DUET OR SEMI-CHORUS.

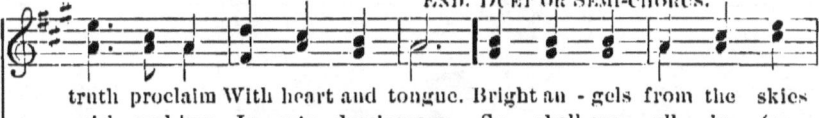

truth proclaim With heart and tongue. Bright an - gels from the skies
girl and boy In wis - dom's ways: So shall we all be free

D.C.

Look down with gladsome eyes When Thy sweet prais - es rise By chil-dren sung.
From sin and mis - er - y, And heav'n our home shall be; Thine all the praise.

253 Palms of Glory.

J. MONTGOMERY.   Arr. from Schon. By per.

1. Palms of glo-ry, rai-ment bright, Crowns, that nev-er fade a-way.
Gird and deck the saints in light, Priests, and kings, and con-q'rors they:
Yet the con-q'rors bring their palms To the Lamb a-midst the throne,
And pro-claim in joy-ful psalms, Vict'ry thro' His cross a-lone.

2 Kings for harps their crowns resign,
  Crying, as they strike the chords,
"Take the kingdom — it is Thine,—
  King of kings, and Lord of lords!"
Round the altar, priests confess,—
  If their robes are white as snow,
'Twas the Saviour's righteousness,
  And His blood that made them so.

3 Who were these? — on earth they dwelt,
  Sinners once of Adam's race,
Guilt, and fear, and suff'ring felt,
  But were saved by sov'reign grace;
They were mortal, too, like us;
  Ah! when we like them must die,
May our souls, translated thus,
  Triumph, reign, and shine on high.

254. Spread Thy Wings.

Arr. from the Scotch. By per.

1. What is life? 'Tis but a va-por; Soon it van-ish-es a-way: Life is but a dy-ing ta-per; O my soul, why wish to stay?
2. See that glo-ry, how re-splendent! Brighter far than fan-cy paints; There, in maj-es-ty tran-scendent, Jesus reigns, the King of saints.

CHORUS.
Spread thy wings, spread thy wings, Spread thy wings, my soul, and fly;
Spread thy wings, spread thy wings, Spread thy wings and fly.

3 Joyful crowds His throne surrounding,
Sing with rapture of His love;
Through the heav'ns His praises sounding,
Filling all His courts above. Cho.

4 Go, and share His people's glory;
'Mid the ransomed crowd appear;
Thine's a joyful, wondrous story,
One that angels love to hear. Cho

256. Good Tidings.

KARL REDEN. By per.

1. Shout the ti-dings of sal-va-tion To the a-ged and the young;
2. Shout the ti-dings of sal-va-tion O'er the prairies of the West;
3. Shout the ti-dings of sal-va-tion Mingling with the ocean's roar;

Till the precious in-vi-ta-tion Wak-en ev'ry heart and tongue.
Till each gath'ring con-gre-ga-tion With the gospel sound is blest.
Till the ships of ev-'ry na-tion Bear the news from shore to shore.

CHORUS.
Send the sound The earth a-round, Send the sound The earth around.
Send the sound, Send the sound The earth a-round.

4 Shout the tidings of salvation
O'er the islands of the sea;
Till, in humble adoration,
All to Christ shall bow the knee.
Cho.

5 Shout the tidings of salvation,
Till the world shall hear the call;
And with joyous acclamation,
Crown the Saviour Lord of all.
Cho.

257 Can You Delay?

E. C. Revons. By per.

1. The Saviour calls—let ev-'ry ear At-tend the heavenly sound; Ye doubt-ing souls, dis-miss your fear; Hope smiles re-viv-ing sound.
2. For ev-'ry thirst-y, long-ing heart, Here streams of bounty flow; And life and health and bliss im-part, To ban-ish mor-tal woe.

CHORUS.
Ye sin-ners, come—'tis mer-cy's voice; That gracious voice o-bey! Mer-cy in-vites to heav'n-ly joys, And can you yet de-lay? And can you yet de-lay?

3 Here springs of sacred pleasure rise,
To ease your every pain;
Immortal fountain! full supplies!
Nor shall you thirst in vain. Cho.

4 Dear Saviour, draw reluctant hearts;
To Thee let sinners fly;
And take the bliss Thy love imparts,
And drink and never die. Cho.

258. I Love the Sacred Book.

T. KELLY.   C. C. CONVERSE. By per.

1. I love the sa-cred book of God: No oth-er can its place sup-ply; It points me to the saints' a-bode; It gives me wings, and bids me fly.

2 Sweet book! in thee mine eyes discern
The image of my absent Lord;
From thine illumined page I learn
The joys His presence will afford.

3 In thee I "read my title clear
To mansions" that will ne'er decay;
My Lord!—Oh! when will He appear,
And bear His pris'ner far away?

4 But, while I'm here, thou shalt supply
His place, and tell me of His love;
I'll read with faith's discerning eye,
And get a taste of joys above.

5 I know His Spirit breathes in thee,
To animate His people here;
May thy sweet truths prove life to me,
Till in His presence I appear.

259. The Seasons.

DUET.   LESTA VESE. By per.

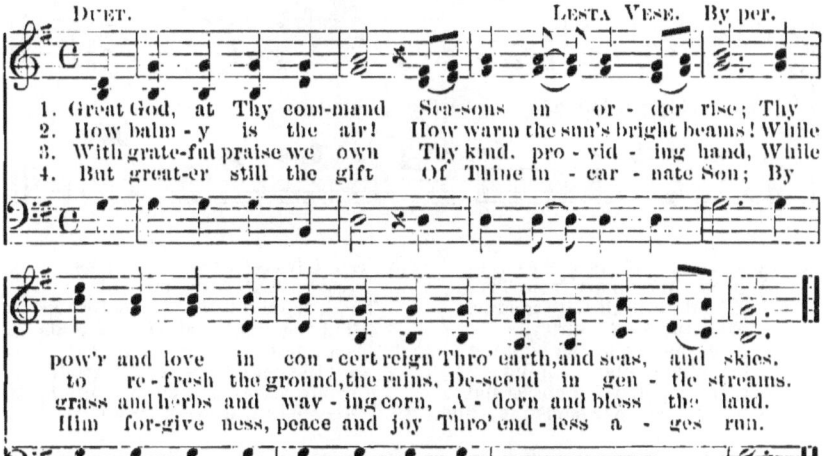

1. Great God, at Thy com-mand Sea-sons in or-der rise; Thy pow'r and love in con-cert reign Thro' earth, and seas, and skies.
2. How balm-y is the air! How warm the sun's bright beams! While to re-fresh the ground, the rains, De-scend in gen-tle streams.
3. With grate-ful praise we own Thy kind, pro-vid-ing hand, While grass and herbs and wav-ing corn, A-dorn and bless the land.
4. But great-er still the gift Of Thine in-car-nate Son; By Him for-give ness, peace and joy Thro' end-less a-ges run.

260. Jesus, Save Us.

H. Bateman.   Arr. from Linley. By per.

1. Jesus! Jesus! come and save us From the sins that so distress,
Make us all Thy love would have us, Happy, in our trustfulness.
Jesus! Jesus! cheering, healing, By the Holy Spirit's aid,
Come, Thy pard'ning love revealing; So we will not be afraid.

2 Jesus! Jesus! life is sadness,
   When it lives apart from Thee;
Come, and fill it all with gladness,
   Pleasantness and purity.
Jesus! Jesus! grant the blessing
   Of a calm, contented mind,
That, the joy of faith possessing,
   Perfect peace our souls may find.

3 Jesus! Jesus! watching o'er us,
   Lead us safely on our way,
Thou, the light of hope, before us,
   Till the night shall change to-day.
Jesus! Jesus! gently guiding
   By the path Thyself hath trod,
For our ceaseless need providing,
   Keep us till we rest with God.

261. Come, Little Children.

262. The Dearest Name.

F. WHITFIELD. — C. C. CONVERSE. By per.

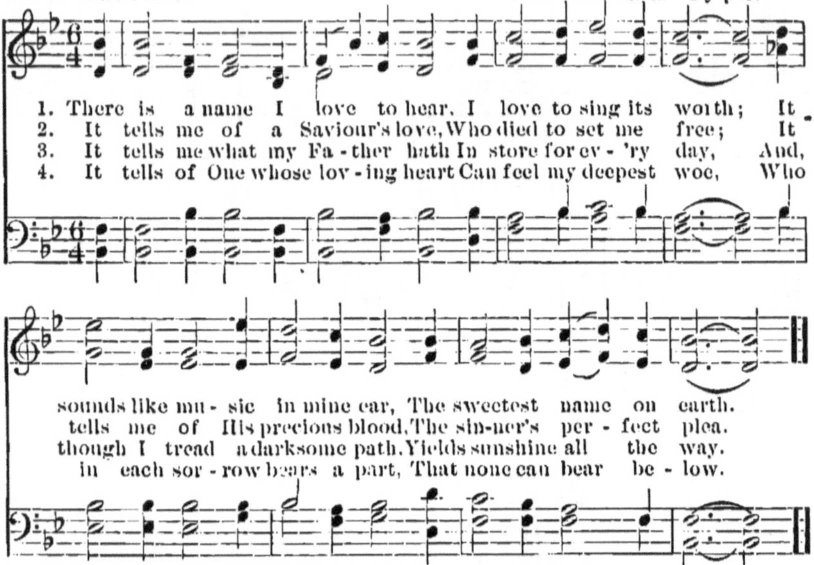

1. There is a name I love to hear, I love to sing its worth; It sounds like mu-sic in mine ear, The sweetest name on earth.
2. It tells me of a Saviour's love, Who died to set me free; It tells me of His precious blood, The sin-ner's per-fect plea.
3. It tells me what my Fa-ther hath In store for ev-'ry day, And, though I tread a darksome path, Yields sunshine all the way.
4. It tells of One whose lov-ing heart Can feel my deepest woe, Who in each sor-row bears a part, That none can bear be-low.

263. Siloam's Shady Rill.

DUET. — Arr. from the German. By per.

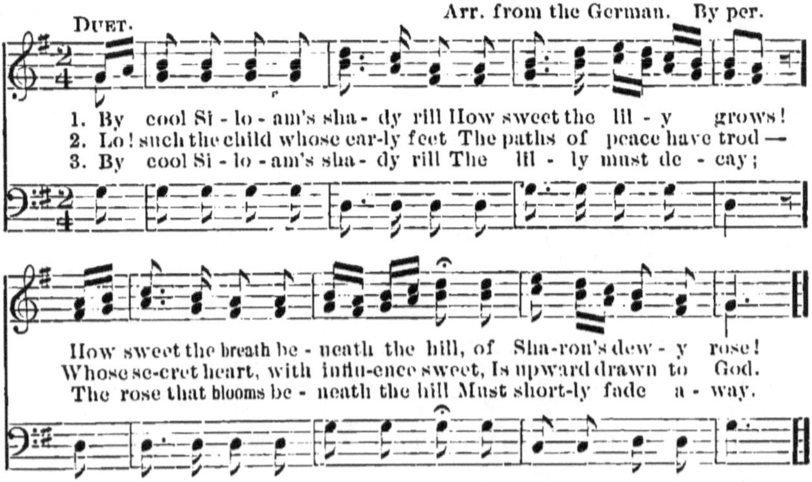

1. By cool Si-lo-am's sha-dy rill How sweet the lil-y grows! How sweet the breath be-neath the hill, of Sha-ron's dew-y rose!
2. Lo! such the child whose ear-ly feet The paths of peace have trod— Whose se-cret heart, with influ-ence sweet, Is upward drawn to God.
3. By cool Si-lo-am's sha-dy rill The lil-ly must de-cay; The rose that blooms be-neath the hill Must short-ly fade a-way.

4 And soon, too soon, the wintry hour
Of man's maturer age [pow'r,
Will shake the soul with sorrow's
And stormy passions rage.

5 O Thou, who givest life and breath,
We seek Thy grace alone, [death,
In childhood, manhood, age, and
To keep us still Thine own.

265 Jerome.

Arr. from the German. By per.

1. High in yon-der realms of light Dwell the rap-tured saints a - bove,
2. 'Mid the cho-rus of the skies,'Mid th' an -gel - ic lyres a - bove,
3. All is tran - quil and se - rene, Calm and un - dis-turbed re - pose;

Far be-yond our fee - ble sight, Hap -py in Im-man -uel's love;—
Hark! their songs melodious rise, Songs of praise to Je - sus' love:
There no cloud can in - ter - vene, There no an - gry tem - pest blows;

Pil -grims in this vale of tears, Once they knew, like us be - low,
Hap -py spir - its, ye are fled Where no grief can en-trance find,—
Ev - 'ry tear is wiped a - way, Sighs no more shall heave the breast;

Gloom -y doubts, dis-tress-ing fears, Torturing pain, and heav -y woe.
Lulled to rest the ach - ing head, Soothed the an -guish of the mind.
Night is lost in end - less day, Sor - row, in e - ter - nal rest.

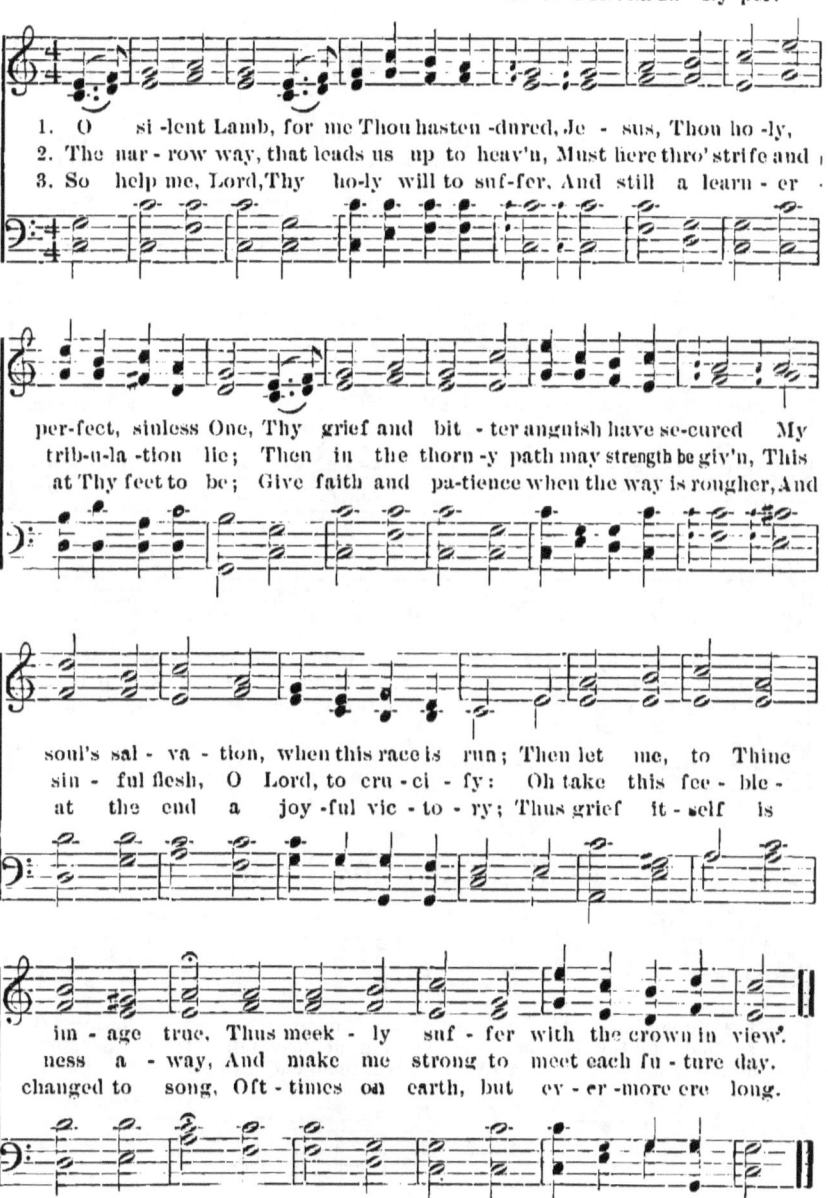

267 Calvary.

C. C. CONVERSE. By per.

1. Near the cross our sta-tion tak-ing, Earth-ly cares and joys for-sak-ing,
2. When no eye its pit - y gave us, When there was no arm to save us,
3. Je - sus, may Thy love con-strain us, That from sin we may re-frain us,

Meet it is for us to mourn; 'T was for us Thou cam'st from heaven,
Thou Thy love and pow'r display'dst; By Thy stripes our help and heal-ing,
In Thy griefs may deep-ly grieve; Thee our best af - fec-tions giv - ing,

'T was for us Thy heart was riv - en,— All Thy griefs for us were borne.
By Thy death our life re-veal - ing, Thou for us the ran - som paid'st.
To Thy praise and hon-or liv - ing, May we in Thy glo - ry live.

268 Chide Mildly the Erring.

S. W. PATTEN. Adapted. By per.

1. Chide mild-ly the err - ing! Kind language en-dears; Grief fol-lows the
2. Chide mild-ly the err - ing! Jeer not at their fall! If strength were but
3. Chide mild-ly the err - ing! Entreat them with care! Their na-tures are

271 Oh for the Robes of Whiteness.

Mrs. C. L. Bancroft. Arr. from Mendelssohn. By per.

1. Oh for the robes of white-ness! Oh for the tear-less eyes! Oh for the glorious bright-ness Of the un-cloud-ed skies! Oh for the no more weep-ing, With-in the land of love, The end-less joy of keep-ing The bri-dal feast a-bove!
2. Oh for the bliss of dy-ing, My ris-en Lord to meet! Oh for the rest of ly-ing For ev-er at His feet! Oh for the hour of see-ing My Sav-iour face to face! The hope of ev-er be-ing In that sweet meet-ing-place!
3. Je-sus, Thou King of glo-ry! I soon shall dwell with Thee; I soon shall sing the sto-ry Of Thy great love to me: Mean-while, my tho'ts shall en-ter E'en now, be-fore Thy throne, That all my love may cen-tre In Thee, and Thee a-lone.

272. Be Firm.

LESTA VESE. By per.

1. Be firm and be faithful; Desert not the right; The brave are the bolder, The darker the night. Then up and be doing, Though foes may assail; Thy duty pursuing, Dare all, and prevail.

2. If scorn be thy portion, If hatred and loss, If stripes or a prison, Remember the cross! God watches above Thee, And He will requite; Stand firm, and be faithful, Desert not the right.

273. Oh! Were I bound in Jesus' Love.

R. WHITTET.   HENRY G. WHITTET. By per.

1. Oh! were I bound in Jesus' love, What joy were mine! what joy were mine! My feet by Him constrained to move, In paths divine, by grace divine. Then would I understand and know, In some degree,—a small degree, How much to His great love I owe, Encircling me,—embracing me!

2 Oh! did the fruits of grace and peace
　Abound in me,—abound in me!
　My soul, O Jesus, could not cease
　　To grow like Thee.— to grow like Thee,
　And then, I know the Comforter
　　Would come to me.—abide with me,
　And witnessing, withdraw my fear
　　Give peace with Thee—sweet peace in Thee.

3 Then send Thy spirit forth with pow'r
　　To keep me true, still ever true,
　And when may come temptation's lure
　　Let slips be few,—give grace anew;
　So will I daily stronger grow
　　When led of Thee, and trained by Thee,
　And from my heart will grateful flow
　　Eternally, sweet praise to Thee.

277 Christ's Incarnation and Advent.

J. Montgomery.   H. Smart.

1. An-gels, from the realms of glo-ry, Wing your flight o'er all the earth,
2. Shepherds, in the field a - bid - ing, Watching o'er your flocks by night,
3. Sa - ges, leave your con-tem-pla-tions, Brighter vi-sions beam a - far;

Ye who sang cre - a - tion's sto-ry, Now proclaim Mes - si - ah's birth;
God with man is now re - sid-ing; Yon-der shines the in - fant-light;
Seek the great De - sire of nations; Ye have seen His na - tal star;

Come and worship, Come and worship, Worship Christ, the new-born King.

4 Saints, before the altar bending,
   Watching long in hope and fear,
Suddenly the Lord, descending,
   In His temple shall appear;
Come and worship,
Worship Christ, the new-born King.

5 Sinners, wrung with true repentance,
   Doomed for guilt to endless pains,
Justice now revokes the sentence;
   Mercy calls you; break your chains;
Come and worship,
Worship Christ, the new-born King.

278 Jesus, Lord of Life Eternal.

Tr. by J. M. Neale.   H. Smart.

1. Je - sus, Lord of life e - ter - nal, Tak-ing those He lov'd the best,
2. Knit is now our flesh to Godhead, Knit in ev - er - last-ing bands;
3. Loos-ing death with all its ter-rors Thou as-cend-ed'st up on high;

JESUS, LORD OF LIFE ETERNAL.

Stood up-on the Mount of Ol - ives, And His own the last time bless'd;
Call the world to high-est fes - tal: Floods and oceans, clap your hands:
And to mor-tals now im-mor-tal, Gav-est im-mor-tal-i - ty,

Then, tho' He had nev - er left it, Sought a-gain His Fa - ther's breast.
An - gels raise the song of tri-umph: Make re-sponse, ye dis - tant lands.
As Thine own dis-ci - ples saw Thee Mounting Vic - tor to the sky.

279   Innocence.
C. WESLEY.   THIBAUT IV.

1. Glo - ry be to God on high, God, whose glo- ry fills the sky;
2. Sov-'reign Fa-ther, heav'n-ly King, Thee we now presume to sing.
3. Hail, by all Thy works a - dored, Hail, the ev - er - last-ing Lord;
4. Christ our Lord and God we own, Christ, the Fa-ther's on-ly Son;

Peace on earth to men for - giv'n, Man, the well-be-lov'd of heav'n.
Glad things at-tri-butes con - fess, Glo-rious all, and num-ber -less.
Thee, with thankful hearts we prove God of pow'r, and God of love.
Lamb of God for sin-ners slain, Sav-iour of of - fend-ing man.

5 Bow Thine ear, in mercy bow:
Hear, the world's atonement Thou:
Jesus, in Thy name we pray,
Take, O take our sins away.

6 Hear, for Thou, O Christ, alone
Art with Thy great Father One;
One, the Holy Ghost with Thee;
One supreme, eternal Three.

280. Christ's Resurrection.

Tr. by J. M. Neale. H. Smart.

1. The day of resurrection, Earth, tell it out abroad:
The Passover of gladness, The Passover of God.
From death to life eternal, From earth unto the sky,
Our Christ hath bro't us over, With hymns of victory.

2 Our hearts be pure from evil,
  That we may see aright
The Lord in rays eternal
  Of resurrection light;
And, list'ning to His accents,
  May hear so calm and plain,
His own "All hail!" and hearing,
  May raise the victor-strain.

3 Now let the heav'ns be joyful;
  Let earth her song begin;
Let the round world keep triumph,
  And all that is therein;
Invisible and visible,
  Their notes let all things blend,
For Christ the Lord hath risen,
  Our Joy that hath no end.

281. Christ's Ascension.

C. WORDSWORTH.   H. SMART.

1. See, the Con-q'ror mounts in triumph, See the King in roy-al state, Rid-ing on the clouds His char-iot To His heav'nly pal-ace gate; Hark! the choirs of an-gel voi-ces Joy-ful hal-le-lu-jahs sing, And the por-tals high are lift-ed, To re-ceive their heav'n-ly King.

2. Who is this that comes in glo-ry, With the trump of ju-bi-lee? Lord of bat-tles, God of ar-mies, He has gain'd the vic-to-ry; He who on the cross did suf-fer, He who from the grave a-rose, He has vanquished sin and Sa-tan, He by death has spoiled His foes.

3. Thou hast raised our human na-ture On the clouds to God's right hand, There we sit in heav'n-ly pla-ces, There with Thee in glo-ry stand; Je-sus reigns a-dored by an-gels, Man with God is on the throne, Might-y Lord, in Thine as-cen-sion We by faith be-hold our own.

4 Lift us up from earth to heaven,
  Give us wings of faith and love,
  Gales of holy aspiration
    Wafting us to realms above;
That, with hearts and minds uplifted,
  We with Christ our Lord may dwell
Where He sits enthroned in glory
    In the heav'nly citadel.

5 So at last, when He appeareth,
  We from out our graves may spring
With our youth renewed like eagles'
    Flocking round our heav'nly King,
Caught up on the clouds of heaven,
  And may meet Him in the air,
Rise to realms where He is reigning,
    And may reign forever there.

285. Pass me not.

Used by permission of W. H. Doane, owner of copyright.

3 Trusting only in Thy merit,
　Would I seek Thy face;
Heal my wounded, broken spirit,
　Save me by Thy grace. Cho.

4 Thou the Spring of all my comfort,
　More than life to me,
Whom have I on earth beside Thee?
　Whom in heaven but Thee? Cho.

STAND UP FOR JESUS.

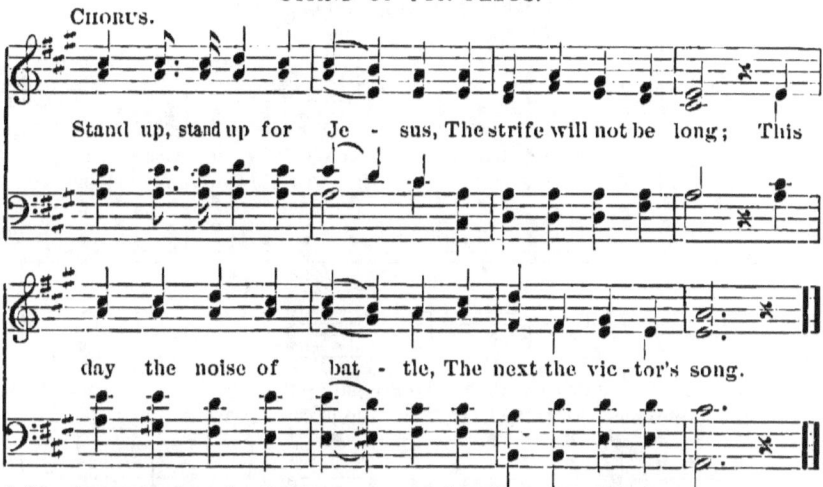

2 Stand up, stand up for Jesus,
  The trumpet call obey;
  Forth to the mighty conflict,
  In this His glorious day:
  Ye that are men! now serve Him,
  Against unnumbered foes;
  Your courage rise with danger,
  And strength to strength oppose.

3 Stand up, stand up for Jesus;
  Stand in His strength alone;
  The arm of flesh will fail you;
  Ye dare not trust your own:
  Put on the gospel armor,
  And, watching unto prayer,
  Where duty calls, or danger,
  Be never wanting there.

287   O thou Heir of Heaven.

Arr. from WEBER. By per.

2 Think of Calv'ry's mountain,
  Where His blood was spilt;
  In that precious fountain
  Wash away thy guilt.
  Set the prize before thee;
  Gird thy armor on:
  Heir of grace and glory,
  Struggle for thy crown.

291 Charity.

Adapted from STEPHEN GLOVER. By per.

CHARITY.

2 Hoping ever, failing never,
　　Tho' deceived, believing still;
Long abiding, all confiding,
　　To thy heav'nly Father's will:
Never weary of welldoing,
　　Never fearful of the end;
Claiming all mankind as brothers,
　　Thou dost all alike befriend.

293. The Galilean King.

Rev. R. P. Kerr, D. D. Rev. R. P. Kerr, D. D. By per.

1. Gal-i-le-an King and Prophet, Thou who once be-strode the sea,
2. Gal-i-le-an King and Shepherd, Who Thy flock didst gently lead,
3. Gal-i-le-an King and Heal-er! There are ma-ny wait-ing here,
4. Gal-i-le-an King and Sav-iour! Here we crave Thy pard'ning grace;

Come a-cross the troubled wa-ters, Come and bid our sor-rows flee;
Thro' the fields and by the sea-side, Now Thy sheep on mer-cies feed.
Wait-ing with their wounded spir-its Speak-ing but with sigh or tear;
Wilt Thou not for-give us free-ly As we kneel be-fore Thy face?

Let us hear the might-y man-date Of Thine own re-sist-less will;
In the moun-tains and the des-ert, As the thousands followed Thee;
Wilt Thou guide Thy white-wing'd ves-sel Toward the sorrow-sha-ded strand?
Cleansing, righteousness, a-dop-tion, And re-new-ing from Thy love,

Call-ing calm-ness o'er the tem-pest, Let us hear Thy "peace be still."
We, the hun-gry, press the near-est, For Thy boun-ty full and free.
Come, and give new life and bless-ing; Touch us with Thy ten-der hand.
Give us all, that we may serve Thee, Till we find our rest a-bove.

Used by per. of Rev. R. P. Kerr, D. D. owner of Copyright.

294 Blessed Night.

H. BONAR.   C. C. CONVERSE. By per.

1. Bless-ed night, when Bethlem's plain Ech-oed with the joy-ful strain, "Peace has come to earth again" Hal-le-lu - jah!

2 Blessèd hills, that heard the song
Of the glorious angel throng
Swelling all your slopes along;
Hallelujah!
3 Happy shepherd, on whose ear,
Fell the tidings glad and clear,
" God to man is drawing near."
Hallelujah!
4 Thus revealed to shepherd's eyes
Hidden from the great and wise,

Ent'ring earth in lowly guise—
Hallelujah!
5 We adore Thee as our King,
And to Thee our song we sing;
Our best off'ring to Thee bring,
Hallelujah!
6 Mighty King of Righteousness,
King of Glory, King of Peace,
Never shall Thy kingdom cease!
Hallelujah!

295 Always with Us.

E. H. NEVIN.   Arr. from L. WELY. By per.

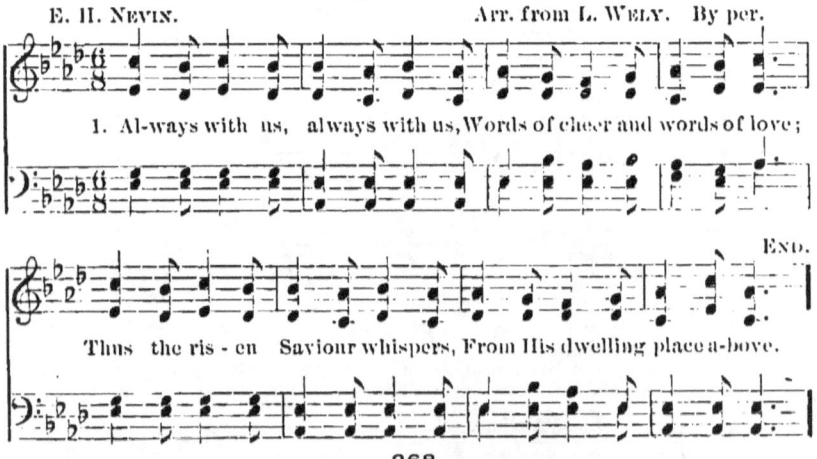

1. Al-ways with us, always with us, Words of cheer and words of love;
Thus the ris-en Saviour whispers, From His dwelling place a-bove.

ALWAYS WITH US.

With us when we toil in sadness, Sowing much and reaping none;
Tell-ing us that in the future Golden harvests shall be won.

2 With us when the storm is sweeping
   O'er our pathway dark and drear;
   Waking hope within our bosoms,
   Stilling ev'ry anxious fear.

With us in the lonely valley,
   When we cross the chilling stream;
   Lighting up the steps to glory
   With salvation's radiant beam.

296   All is Well.

MARY B. PETERS.   Arr. from FLOTOW. By per.

1. Thro' the love of God our Sav-iour, All will be well, All will be well;
2. Tho' we pass through tri-bu-la-tion, All will be well, All will be well:

Free and changeless is His fa - vor; All, all is well, All, all is well.
Ours is such a full sal - va - tion, All, all is well, All, all is well.

D.C. *Strong the hand stretched out to shield us, All must be well, All must be well.*
D.C. *Ho-ly, through the Spir-it's guid-ing, All must be well, All must be well.*

Precious is the blood that heal'd us, Per-fect is the grace that seal'd us;
Hap-py, still in God con - fid - ing, Fruit-ful, if in Christ a - bid - ing,

THAT THOU WILT PLEAD FOR ME.

298. Jesus, Saviour, Look on Me.

C. ELLIOTT.   Rev. ROBERT P. KERR, D.D. By per.

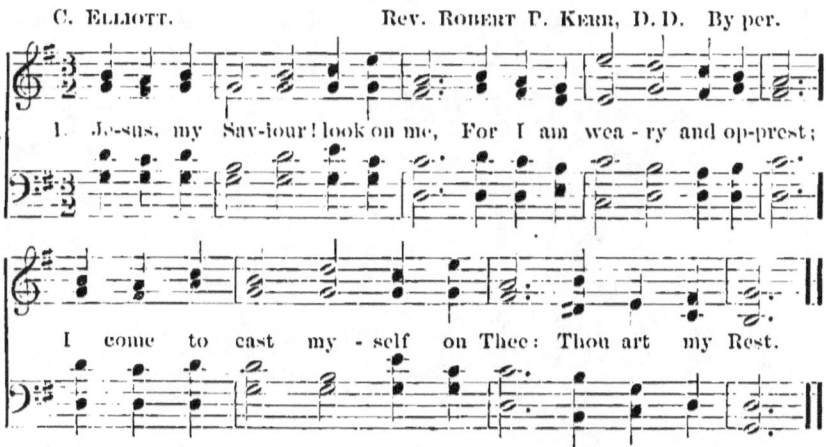

2 Look down on me, for I am weak;
   I feel the toilsome journey's length;
  From Thee, almighty aid I seek :
    Thou art my Strength.

3 I am bewilder'd on my way;
   Dark and tempestuous is the night;
  Oh, send Thou forth some cheering [ray!
    Thou art my Light.

4 Standing alone on Jordan's brink,
   In that tremendous latest strife,
  Thou wilt not suffer me to sink :
    Thou art my Life.

5 Thou wilt my ev'ry want supply,
   E'en to the end, whate'er befall;
  Through life, in death, eternally,
    Thou art my All.

299 There's a Wideness in God's Mercy.

F. W. Faber.   C. C. Converse. By per.

THERE'S A WIDENESS IN GOD'S MERCY.

Sav-iour, who would have us Come and gath-er round His feet?

2 There's no place where earthly sorrows
  Are more felt than up in Heav'n,
There's no place where earthly failings
  Have such kindly judgment giv'n,
There is welcome for the sinner,
  And more graces for the good;
There is mercy with the Saviour;
  There is healing in His blood. Cho.

3 O! the love of God is broader
  Than the measure of man's mind;
And the heart of the Eternal
  Is most wonderfully kind.
If our love were but more simple,
  We should take Him at His word;
And our lives would be all sunshine
  In the sweetness of our Lord. Cho.

300 Acquaint Thyself with God.

Arr. from BELLINI. By per.

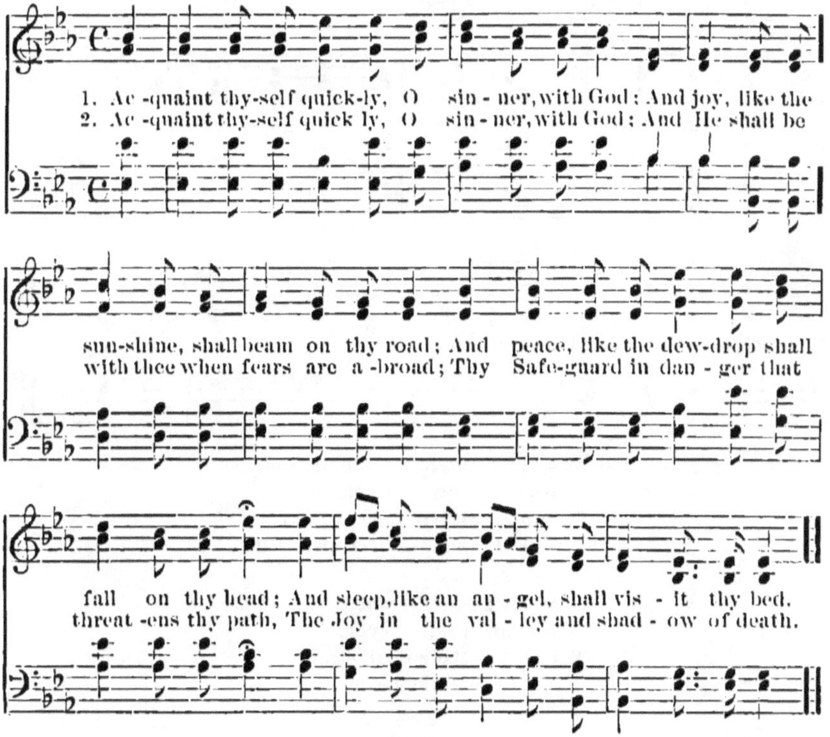

1. Ac-quaint thy-self quick-ly, O sin-ner, with God; And joy, like the sun-shine, shall beam on thy road; And peace, like the dew-drop shall fall on thy head; And sleep, like an an-gel, shall vis-it thy bed.
2. Ac-quaint thy-self quick-ly, O sin-ner, with God; And He shall be with thee when fears are a-broad; Thy Safe-guard in dan-ger that threat-ens thy path, The Joy in the val-ley and shad-ow of death.

301 Near the Cross.

3 Near the Cross! O Lamb of God,
 Bring its scenes before me;
 Help me walk from day to day,
 With its shadows o'er me. Cho.

4 Near the Cross I'll watch and wait,
 Hoping, trusting ever,
 Till I reach the golden strand,
 Just beyond the river. Cho.

302. The Precious Name.

Mrs. Lydia Baxter.   W. H. Doane.

1. Take the name of Je-sus with you, Child of sor-row and of woe—
It will joy and comfort give you, Take it then where'er you go.

2. Take the name of Je-sus ev - er, As a shield from ev'ry snare;
If temp- ta-tions' round you gath - er, Breathe that ho-ly name in pray'r.

CHORUS.

Precious name, O how sweet! Hope of earth and joy of
Precious Name, O how sweet!
heav'n, Precious name, O how sweet—Hope of earth and joy of heav'n.
Precious Name, O how sweet, how sweet,

Copyright, 1871, by Biglow & Main. Used by permission.

3 Oh! the precious name of Jesus;
   How it thrills our souls with joy.
   When His loving arms receive us,
   And His songs our tongues employ! Cho.

4 At the name of Jesus bowing,
   Falling prostrate at His feet,
   King of kings in heav'n we'll crown Him,
   When our journey is complete. Cho.

304 Jacob's Ladder.

305 A Charge to Keep. S. M.

A CHARGE to keep I have,
  A God to glorify;
A never-dying soul to save,
  And fit it for the sky.

2 From youth to hoary age,
  My calling to fulfil:
O may it all my powers engage
  To do my master's will.

3 Arm me with jealous care,
  As in thy sight to live,
And O, thy servant, Lord, prepare
  A strict account to give.

4 Help me to watch and pray,
  And on thyself rely;
Assured if I my trust betray,
  I shall for ever die.

306 Praise for Loving-Kindness. L. M.

AWAKE, my soul, in joyful lays,
And sing thy great Redeemer's praise:
He justly claims a song from thee;
His loving-kindness, O! how free!

2 He saw me ruined in the fall,
Yet loved me notwithstanding all;
He saved me from my lost estate;
His loving-kindness, O! how great!

3 Though numerous hosts of mighty foes,
Though earth and hell my way oppose,
He safely leads my soul along;
His loving-kindness, O! how strong!

4 When trouble, like a gloomy cloud,
Has gathered thick, and thundered loud,
He near my soul has always stood;
His loving-kindness, O! how good!

5 Often I feel my sinful heart
Prone from my Saviour to depart;
But though I oft have him forgot,
His loving-kindness changes not.

6 Soon shall I pass the gloomy vale,
Soon all my mortal powers must fail;
O may my last expiring breath
His loving-kindness sing in death.

7 Then, let me mount and soar away
To the bright world of endless day,
And sing, with rapture and surprise,
His loving-kindness in the skies.

307 Triumphant Grace. C. M.

AMAZING grace! how sweet the sound,
  That saved a wretch like me!
I once was lost, but now am found,
  Was blind, but now I see.

2 'Twas grace that taught my heart to fear,
  And grace my fears relieved;
How precious did that grace appear,
  The hour I first believed!

3 Through many dangers, toils and snares,
  I have already come;
'Tis grace has brought me safe thus far,
  And grace will lead me home.

4 The Lord has promised good to me,
  His word my hope secures;
He will my shield and portion be,
  As long as life endures.

5 And when this flesh and heart shall fail,
  And mortal life shall cease;
I shall possess, within the veil,
  A life of joy and peace.

6 The earth shall soon dissolve like snow,
  The sun forbear to shine;
But God, who called me here below,
  Will be for ever mine.

308 Children Around the Throne.

AROUND the throne of God in heaven,
  Thousands of children stand;
Children whose sins are all forgiven,
  A holy, happy band, [on high.
Singing, glory, glory, glory be to God

2 In flowing robes of spotless white
  See every one arrayed;
Dwelling in everlasting light,
  And joys that never fade,
    Singing, glory, etc.

3 What brought them to that world above,
  That heaven so bright and fair,
Where all is peace and joy and love?
  How came those children there?
    Singing, glory, etc.

4 Because the Saviour shed his blood,
  To wash away their sin;
Bathed in that pure and precious flood,
  Behold them white and clean!
    Singing, glory, etc.

5 On earth they sought the Saviour's grace,
  On earth they loved his name;
So now they see his blessed face,
  And stand before the lamb,
    Singing, glory, etc.

309 BLEST BE THE TIE THAT BINDS

BLEST be the tie that binds
  Our hearts in Christian love;
The fellowship of kindred minds
  Is like to that above.

2 Before our Father's throne,
  We pour our ardent prayers;
Our fears, our hopes, our aims are one,—
  Our comforts and our cares.

3 We share our mutual woes;
  Our mutual burdens bear;
And often for each other flows
  The sympathizing tear.

4 When we asunder part,
  It gives us inward pain,
But we shall still be joined in heart,
  And hope to meet again.

310 PERSEVERANCE. 7s.

CHILDREN of the heavenly King,
  As ye journey, sweetly sing:
Sing your Saviour's worthy praise,
Glorious in his works and ways.

2 Ye are travelling home to God,
  In the way the fathers trod;
They are happy now, and ye
Soon their happiness shall see.

3 O ye mourning souls be glad;
  Christ our Advocate is made;
Us to save, our flesh assumes,
Brother to our soul becomes.

4 Shout ye little flock, and blest,
  Soon you'll enter into rest;
There your seat is now prepared,
There your kingdom and reward.

5 Fear not, brethren, joyful stand
  On the borders of your land;
Jesus Christ, our Father's Son,
Bids us undismayed go on.

6 Lord, submissive make us go,
  Gladly leaving all below,
Only thou our Leader be,
And we still will follow thee.

311 PRAYER FOR THE DESCENT C. M.
           OF THE SPIRIT.

COME, Holy Spirit, heavenly Dove,
  With all thy quickening powers,
Kindle a flame of sacred love
  In these cold hearts of ours.

2 Look how we grovel here below,
  Fond of these trifling toys:
Our souls can neither fly nor go,
  To reach eternal joys.

3 In vain we tune our formal songs,
  In vain we strive to rise;
Hosannas languish on our tongues,
  And our devotion dies.

4 Dear Lord, and shall we ever live
  At this poor dying rate;
Our love so faint, so cold to thee,
  And thine to us so great?

5 Come, Holy Spirit, heavenly Dove,
  With all thy quickening powers;
Come, shed abroad a Saviour's love,
  And that shall kindle ours.

312 GRATEFUL RECOLLECTIONS. 8s & 7s.

COME, thou fount of every blessing,
  Tune my heart to sing thy grace;
Streams of mercy, never ceasing,
  Call for songs of loudest praise.
Teach me some melodious sonnet,
  Sung by flaming tongues above;
Praise the mount—O fix me on it,
  Mount of God's unchanging love.

2 Here I raise my Ebenezer,
  Hither by thy help I'm come;
And I hope by thy good pleasure,
  Safely to arrive at home.
Jesus sought me when a stranger,
  Wandering from the fold of God;
He, to rescue me from danger,
  Interposed with precious blood.

3 Oh! to grace how great a debtor,
  Daily I'm constrained to be;
Let that grace, Lord, like a fetter,
  Bind my wandering heart to thee.
Prone to wander, Lord, I feel it,
  Prone to leave the God I love;
Here's my heart, Lord, take and seal it,
  Seal it from thy courts above.

Songs of the Covenant.

313   Christ our Guide.   8s, 7s & 4s.

GUIDE me, O thou great Jehovah,
   Pilgrim through this barren land;
I am weak, but thou art mighty,
   Hold me with thy powerful hand:
      Bread of heaven,
Feed me, till I want no more.

2 Open now the crystal fountain,
   Whence the healing streams do flow;
Let the fiery, cloudy pillar
   Lead me all my journey through:
      Strong Deliverer,
Be thou still my strength and shield.

3 When I tread the verge of Jordan,
   Bid my anxious fears subside;
Death of death, and hell's destruction,
   Land me safe on Canaan's side:
      Songs of praises
I will ever give to thee.

314   Prayer for the Children   L. M.
             of the Church.

DEAR Saviour, if these lambs should stray
   From thy secure inclosure's bound,
And lured by worldly joys away,
   Among the thoughtless crowd be found;

2 Remember still that they are thine,
   That thy dear sacred name they bear;
Think that the seal of love divine,
   The sign of covenant grace, they wear.

3 In all their erring, sinful years,
   Oh! let them ne'er forgotten be;
Remember all the prayers and tears
   Which made them consecrate to thee.

4 And when these lips no more can pray,
   These eyes can weep for them no more,
Turn thou their feet from folly's ways,
   The wanderers to thy fold restore.

315   Love to Christ.   C. M.

DO not I love thee, O my Lord?
   Behold my heart, and see;
And turn each hateful idol out,
   That dares to rival thee.

2 Do not I love thee from my soul?
   Then let me nothing love:
Dead be my heart to every joy
   Which thou dost not approve.

3 Hast thou a lamb in all thy flock,
   I would disdain to feed?
Hast thou a foe, before whose face,
   I fear thy cause to plead?

4 Thou knowest I love thee, dearest Lord!
   But oh! I long to soar,
Far from the sphere of mortal joys,
   That I may love thee more.

316   A Thankful Heart.   C. M.

FATHER, whate'er of earthly bliss
   Thy sovereign will denies,
Accepted at thy throne of grace,
   Let this petition rise:

2 Give me a calm, a thankful heart,
   From every murmur free;
The blessings of thy grace impart,
   And make me live to thee.

3 Let the sweet hope that thou art mine
   My life and death attend;
Thy presence through my journey shine,
   And crown my journey's end.

317   The Pilgrim.   8s & 7s.

GENTLY, Lord, O gently lead us,
   Through this lonely vale of tears;
Through the changes thou'st decreed us,
   Till our last great change appears.
When temptation's darts assail us,
   When in devious paths we stray,
Let thy goodness never fail us,
   Lead us in thy perfect way.

2 In the hour of pain and anguish,
   In the hour when death draws near,
Suffer not our hearts to languish,
   Suffer not our souls to fear;
And when mortal life is ended,
   Bid us in thine arms to rest,
Till by angel bands attended,
   We awake among the blest.

318   The Mercy-Seat.   L. M.

FROM every stormy wind that blows,
   From every swelling tide of woes,
There is a calm, a sure retreat,
   'Tis found beneath the mercy-seat.

2 There is a place where Jesus sheds
   The oil of gladness on our heads;
A place than all besides more sweet,
   It is the blood-bought mercy-seat.

3 There is a scene, where spirits blend,
  Where friend holds fellowship with friend;
  Though sundered far, by faith they meet,
  Around one common mercy-seat.

4 Ah! whither could we flee for aid,
  When tempted, desolate, dismayed?
  Or how the hosts of hell defeat,
  Had suffering saints no mercy-seat?

5 There, there on eagles' wings we soar,
  And sin and sense seem all no more;
  And heaven comes down our souls to greet,
  And glory crowns the mercy-seat.

6 Oh! let my hand forget her skill,
  My tongue be silent, cold, and still,
  This bounding heart forget to beat,
  If I forget thy mercy-seat.

319   MISSIONARY HYMN.   7s & 6s.

FROM Greenland's icy mountains,
  From India's coral strand;
Where Afric's sunny fountains
  Roll down their golden sand;
From many an ancient river,
  From many a palmy plain,
They call us to deliver
  Their land from error's chain.

2 What, though the spicy breezes
  Blow soft o'er Ceylon's isle,
Though every prospect pleases,
  And only man is vile;
In vain, with lavish kindness,
  The gifts of God are strown;
The heathen, in his blindness,
  Bows down to wood and stone.

3 Shall we, whose souls are lighted
  With wisdom from on high,
Shall we, to men benighted,
  The lamp of life deny?
Salvation! O salvation!
  The joyful sound proclaim,
Till earth's remotest nation
  Has learned Messiah's name.

4 Waft, waft, ye winds, his story,
  And you, ye waters, roll,
Till, like a sea of glory,
  It spreads from pole to pole;
Till o'er our ransomed nature,
  The lamb for sinners slain,
Redeemer, King, Creator,
  In bliss returns to reign.

320   CHRIST'S KINGDOM.   8s & 7s.

HARK! ten thousand harps and voices
  Sound the note of praise above;
Jesus reigns and heav'n rejoices,
  Jesus reigns, the God of love:
See, he sits on yonder throne,—
  Jesus rules the world alone.

2 Saviour, hasten thine appearing—
  Bring, oh! bring the glorious day,
When, the awful summons hearing,
  Heav'n and earth shall pass away;
Then, with angel choirs, we'll sing,
  "Glory, glory to our king."

321   THE LORD IS RISEN—HE LIVES AGAIN.   C. H. M.

HOW calm and beautiful the morn
  That gilds the sacred tomb,
Where once the crucified was borne,
  And veiled in midnight gloom!
O weep no more the Saviour slain,
The Lord is ris'n—he lives again!

2 Ye mourning saints, dry every tear
  For your departed Lord!
"Behold the place—he is not here,"
  The tomb is all unbarred:
The gates of death were closed in vain,
The Lord is ris'n—he lives again!

3 Now cheerful to the house of prayer
  Your early footsteps bend,
The Saviour will himself be there,
  Your Advocate and Friend:
Once by the law your hopes were slain,
But now in Christ ye live again.

4 How tranquil now the rising day!
  'Tis Jesus still appears,
A risen Lord, to chase away
  Your unbelieving fears:
Oh, weep no more your comforts slain,
The Lord is ris'n—he lives again!

322   THE SABBATH A DELIGHT.   S. M.

WELCOME, sweet day of rest,
  That saw the Lord arise;
Welcome to this reviving breast,
  And these rejoicing eyes.

2 The King himself comes near,
  And feasts his saints to-day;
Here we may sit, and see him here,
  And love and praise and pray.

3 My willing soul would stay
 In such a frame as this,
 And sit and sing herself away
 To everlasting bliss.

323   The Promises Precious.   11s.

HOW firm a foundation, ye saints of
  the Lord,
Is laid for your faith in his excellent
  word!
What more can he say than to you he
  hath said,
You who unto Jesus for refuge have
  fled?

2 In every condition, in sickness, in
   health,
 In poverty's vale, or abounding in wealth,
 At home and abroad, on the land, on the
   sea,
 "As thy days may demand, shall thy
   strength ever be.

3 "Fear not, I am with thee, O be not dis-
    mayed,
 I, I am thy God, and will still give thee
   aid;
 I'll strengthen thee, help thee, and cause
   thee to stand,
 Upheld by my righteous, omnipotent
   hand.

4 "When through the deep waters I call
    thee to go,
 The rivers of woe shall not thee over-
   flow;
 For I will be with thee, thy troubles to
   bless
 And sanctify to thee, thy deepest distress.

5 "When through fiery trials thy pathway
    shall lie,
 My grace all-sufficient shall be thy supply;
 The flame shall not hurt thee; I only
   design
 Thy dross to consume, and thy gold to
   refine.

6 "E'en down to old age, all my people
    shall prove
 My sovereign, eternal, unchangeable
   love;
 And when hoary hairs shall their tem-
   ples adorn,
 Like lambs they shall still in my bosom
   be borne.

7 "The soul that on Jesus hath leaned for
    repose,
 I will not, I will not desert to his foes;
 That soul, though all hell should en-
   deavor to shake,
 I'll never, no never, no never forsake."

924   Love to Christ.   C. M.

HOW sweet the name of Jesus sounds
  In a believer's ear!
It soothes his sorrows, heals his wounds,
  And drives away his fear.

2 It makes the wounded spirit whole,
   And calms the troubled breast;
 'Tis manna to the hungry soul,
   And to the weary, rest.

3 Dear Name, the rock on which I build,
   My shield and hiding-place;
 My never-failing treasury filled
   With boundless stores of grace!

4 Jesus, my Shepherd, Husband, Friend,
   My Prophet, Priest, and King;
 My Lord, my Life, my Way, my End,
   Accept the praise I bring.

5 Weak is the effort of my heart,
   And cold my warmest thought;
 But when I see thee as thou art,
   I'll praise thee as I ought.

6 Till then I would thy love proclaim
   With every fleeting breath;
 And may the music of thy name.
   Refresh my soul in death.

325   The Voice of Jesus.   8s & 6s.

I HEARD the voice of Jesus say,
   Come unto me and rest;
 Lay down, thou weary one, lay down
   Thy head upon my breast.
 I came to Jesus as I was,
   Weary, and worn, and sad,
 I found in him a resting-place,
   And he has made me glad.

2 I heard the voice of Jesus say,
   Behold, I freely give
 The living water: thirsty one,
   Stoop down, and drink, and live.
 I came to Jesus, and I drank
   Of that life-giving stream;
 My thirst was quenched, my soul revived,
   And now I live in him.

SONGS OF THE COVENANT.

3 I heard the voice of Jesus say,
  I am this dark world's light,—
Look unto me, thy morn shall rise,
  And all thy day be bright:
I looked to see Jesus, and I found
  In him my Star, my Sun;
And in that light of life I'll walk,
  Till travelling days are done.

4 I heard the voice of Jesus say,
  My Father's house above
Has many mansions: I've a place
  Prepared for you in love.
I trust in Jesus:—in that house,
  According to his word,
Redeemed by grace, my soul shall live
  For ever with the Lord.

326   THE CHRISTIAN PILGRIM.   10s, 11s.

I'M a pilgrim, and I'm a stranger;
  I can tarry, I can tarry but a night;
Do not detain me, for I am going
  To where the fountains are ever flowing.
I'm a pilgrim, and I'm a stranger,
  I can tarry, I can tarry but a night.

2 There the sunbeams are ever shining,
  I am longing, I am longing for the sight.
Within a country, unknown and dreary,
  I have been wandering forlorn and weary.
    I'm a pilgrim, etc.

3 Of that country, to which I'm going,
  My Redeemer, my Redeemer is the light;
There are no sorrows, nor any sighing,
  Nor any sin there, nor any dying.
    I'm a pilgrim, etc.

327   REST FOR THE WEARY.   P. M.

IN the Christian's home in glory
  There remains a land of rest,
There my Saviour's gone before me,
  To fulfil my soul's request.
    There is rest for the weary,
      There is rest for you;
    On the other side of Jordan,
      In the sweet fields of Eden,
    Where the tree of life is blooming,
      There is rest for you.

2 This is not my place of resting,
  Mine's a city yet to come;
Onward to it I am hasting,
  On to my eternal home:
    There is rest, etc.

3 In it all is light and glory,
  O'er it shines a nightless day;
Ev'ry trace of sin's sad story,
  All the curse hath passed away:
    There is rest, etc.

4 There the Lamb, our Shepherd, leads us
  By the streams of life along,
On the freshest pastures feeds us,
  Turns our sighing into song:
    There is rest, etc.

328   THE NEW JERUSALEM.   C. M.

JERUSALEM, my happy home,
  Name ever dear to me!
When shall my labors have an end
  In joy and peace, and thee?

2 When shall these eyes thy heaven-built walls
  And pearly gates behold?
Thy bulwarks, with salvation strong,
  And streets of shining gold?

3 Oh! when, thou city of my God,
  Shall I thy courts ascend,
Where congregations ne'er break up,
  And Sabbaths have no end?

4 There happier bowers than Eden's bloom,
  Nor sin nor sorrow know:
Blest seats, through rude and stormy scenes,
  I onward press to you.

5 Why should I shrink at pain and woe,
  Or feel at death dismay?
I've Canaan's goodly land in view,
  And realms of endless day.

6 Apostles, martyrs, prophets there
  Around my Saviour stand;
And soon my friends in Christ below
  Will join the glorious band.

7 Jerusalem, my happy home,
  My soul still pants for thee;
Then shall my labors have an end,
  When I thy joys shall see.

329   WORLD RENOUNCED.   8s. & 7s.

JESUS, I my cross have taken,
  All to leave and follow thee;
Naked, poor, despised, forsaken,
  Thou from hence my all shall be:

Let the world neglect and leave me;
 They have left my Saviour too:
Human hopes have oft deceived me,
 Thou art faithful, thou art true.

2 Perish, earthly fame and treasure,
 Come, disaster, scorn and pain:
In thy service, pain is pleasure:
 With thy favor, loss is gain:
Oh! 'tis not in grief to harm me,
 While thy bleeding love I see;
Oh! 'tis not in joy to charm me,
 When that love is hid from me.

330   Glory of Christ.   C. M.

MAJESTIC sweetness sits enthroned
 Upon the Saviour's brow;
His head with radiant glories crowned,
 His lips with grace o'erflow.

2 No mortal can with him compare
 Among the sons of men;
Fairer is he than all the fair,
 Who fill the heavenly train.

3 He saw me plunged in deep distress,
 And flew to my relief;
For me he bore the shameful cross,
 And carried all my grief.

4 To him I owe my life and breath,
 And all the joys I have;
He makes me triumph over death,
 And saves me from the grave.

5 To heaven, the place of his abode,
 He brings my weary feet,
Shows me the glories of my God,
 And makes my joys complete.

6 Since from his bounty I receive
 Such proofs of love divine,
Had I a thousand hearts to give,
 Lord, they should all be thine.

331   Mary at the Tomb.   7s.

MARY to the Saviour's tomb,
 Hasted at the early dawn;
Spice she brought and sweet perfume,
 But the Lord she loved had gone:
For awhile she lingering stood,
 Filled with sorrow and surprise,
Trembling, while a crystal flood
 Issued from her weeping eyes.

2 But her sorrows quickly fled,
 When she heard his welcome voice:
Christ had risen from the dead,
 Now he bids her heart rejoice:
What a change his word can make,
 Turning darkness into day!
Ye who weep for Jesus' sake,
 He will wipe your tears away.

332   Bearing the Cross.   C. M.

MUST Jesus bear the cross alone,
 And all the world go free?
No, there's a cross for every one,
 And there's a cross for me.

2 The consecrated cross I'll bear,
 Till death shall set me free,
And then go home, my crown to wear,
 For there's a crown for me

333   Jesus Abide with Me.   L. M.

SUN of my soul, thou Saviour dear,
 It is not night if thou be near:
Oh! may no earth-born cloud arise,
To hide thee from thy servant's eyes.

2 When soft the dews of kindly sleep
My wearied eyelids gently steep,
Be my last thought—how sweet to rest
For ever on my Saviour's breast.

3 Abide with me from morn till eve,
For without thee I cannot live;
Abide with me when night is nigh,
For without thee I dare not die.

4 Be near to bless me when I wake,
Ere through the world my way I take;
Abide with me till, in thy love,
I lose myself in heaven above.

334   Sitting at the Foot of the Cross.   8s & 7s.

SWEET the moments, rich in blessing,
 Which before the cross I spend,
Life and health and peace possessing,
 From the sinner's dying Friend.

2 Here I'll sit for ever viewing,
 Mercy flow in streams of blood;
Precious drops, my soul bedewing,
 Plead and claim my peace with God.

3 Truly blessed is this station,
   Low before his cross to lie;
  While I see divine compassion
   Floating in his languid eye.

4 Here it is I find my heaven,
   While upon the cross I gaze;
  Love I much? I'm much forgiven,
   I'm a miracle of grace.

5 Love and grief my heart dividing,
   With my tears, his feet I bathe;
  Constant still in faith abiding,
   Life deriving from his death.

335   SALVATION BY THE BLOOD   C. M.
            OF THE LAMB.

THERE is a fountain filled with blood,
   Drawn from Immanuel's veins:
And sinners plunged beneath that flood,
   Lose all their guilty stains.

2 The dying thief rejoiced to see
   That fountain in his day;
  And there may I, though vile as he,
   Wash all my sins away.

3 Dear dying Lamb, thy precious blood
   Shall never lose its power,
  Till all the ransomed church of God
   Be saved to sin no more.

4 E'er since by faith I saw the stream,
   Thy flowing wounds supply,
  Redeeming love has been my theme,
   And shall be till I die.

5 Then in a nobler, sweeter song,
   I'll sing thy power to save;
  When this poor lisping, stammering tongue
   Lies silent in the grave.

336   EVENING HYMN.   L. M.

THUS far the Lord has led me on,
   Thus far his power prolongs my days,
And every evening shall make known
   Some fresh memorial of his grace.

2 Much of my time has run to waste,
   And I, perhaps, am near my home;
  But he forgives my follies past;
   He gives me strength for days to come.

3 I lay my body down to sleep,
   Peace is the pillow for my head;
  While well appointed angels keep
   Their watchful stations round my bed.

4 Thus when the night of death shall come
   My flesh shall rest beneath the ground;
  And wait thy voice to rouse the tomb,
   With sweet salvation in the sound.

337   VALUE OF PRESENT TIME.   S. M.

TO-MORROW, Lord, is thine,
   Lodged in thy sovereign hand,
And if its sun arise and shine,
   It shines by thy command.

2 The present moment flies,
   And bears our life away;
  O make thy servants truly wise,
   That they may live to-day.

3 Since on this winged hour
   Eternity is hung,
  Waken by thy almighty power
   The aged and the young.

4 One thing demands our care;
   O be it still pursued,
  Lest, slighted once, the season fair
   Should never be renewed.

5 To Jesus may we fly,
   Swift as the morning light,
  Lest life's young golden beam should die
   In sudden, endless night.

338   HAPPY LAND.   6s, 4s.

THERE is a happy land,
   Far, far away,
Where saints in glory stand,
   Bright, bright as day;
Oh! how they sweetly sing,
Worthy is our Saviour King.
Loud let his praises ring,
   Praise, praise for aye.

2 Come to that happy land,
   Come, come away;
Why will ye doubting stand,
   Why still delay?
Oh! we shall happy be,
When from sin and sorrow free,
Lord, we shall live with thee,
   Blest, blest for aye.

3 Bright, in that happy land,
   Beams every eye;
Kept by a Father's hand,
   Love cannot die.

  Oh! then to glory run,
  Be a crown and kingdom won,
  And bright above the sun,
   We reign for aye.

339 The Rest of Heaven. C. M. D.

THERE is an hour of peaceful rest,
 To mourning wanderers given;
There is a joy for souls distrest,
A balm for every wounded breast,
 'Tis found above—in heaven.

2 There is a home for weary souls,
 By sin and sorrow driven;
When tossed on life's tempestuous shoals,
Where storms arise, and ocean rolls,
 And all is drear but heaven.

3 There, faith lifts up her cheerful eye,
 To brighter prospects given;
And views the tempest passing by,
The evening shadows quickly fly,
 And all serene in heaven.

4 There fragrant flowers immortal bloom,
 And joys supreme are given;
There rays divine disperse the gloom—
Beyond the confines of the tomb
 Appears the dawn of heaven.

340 For ever with the Lord. S. M.

"FOR ever with the Lord!"
 Amen; so let it be;
Life from the dead is in that word,
 'Tis immortality.

2 Here in the body pent,
 Absent from him I roam,
Yet nightly pitch my moving tent
 A day's march nearer home.

3 My Father's house on high,
 Home of my soul, how near,
At times, to faith's far-seeing eye,
 Thy golden gates appear!

4 "For ever with the Lord!"
 Father, if 'tis thy will,
The promise of that faithful word,
 Even here to me fulfil.

5 So when my latest breath,
 Shall rend the veil in twain,
By death I shall escape from death,
 And life eternal gain.

6 Knowing as I am known,
 How shall I love that word,
And oft repeat before the throne,
 "For ever with the Lord!"

INDEX OF FIRST LINES.

	Page.
Abide with me,	73
Across the desert's burning sand,	213
Acquaint thyself quickly,	273
A crowd of happy children,	169
A charge to keep I have,	278
A few more years shall roll,	170
A mighty fortress,	104
All hail the power of Jesus' name,	122
All for Jesus,	201
Always with us,	268
Amazing grace, how sweet the sound,	278
And is it true,	40
Angel voices, ever singing,	30
Angels, roll the rock away,	117
Angels from the realms of glory,	252
Approach, my soul,	140
Are you coming to Jesus,	78
Around the throne of God in heaven,	278
As Jacob with travel,	277
Asleep in Jesus,	160
Awake, awake,	62
Awake, my soul, to joyful lays,	278
Be firm and be faithful,	248
Begone, unbelief,	175
Behold, a stranger's at the door,	220
Be kind to each other,	161
Blessing and honor,	167
Blest be the tie that binds,	279
Blessed night, when Bethlem's plain,	268
Book of grace,	176
Brightly gleams our banner,	38
Brief life is here our portion,	93
Brother, rest,	45
Brother, take thy cross,	39
Brother, you may work,	162
Brothers, sing,	217
By cool Siloam's shady rill,	240

	Page.
Chide mildly,	244
Children, listen to the Lord,	216
Children of the heavenly king,	279
Christ for the world we sing,	234
Christ the Lord is risen to-day,	120
Come, Jesus Redeemer,	141
Come, little children,	239
Come, let us sing of Jesus,	80
Come, children, come to God,	205
Come to Jesus,	177
Come, ye saints,	118
Come, ye thankful people,	99
Come to Jesus, little one,	173
Come, let our voices raise,	165
Come and hear the grand old story,	24
Come, said Jesus' sacred voice,	129
Come, Holy Spirit, heavenly Dove,	279
Come, thou fount of every blessing,	279
Commit, thou, all thy griefs,	147
Crown him with many crowns,	42
Courage, brother,	70
Dear Saviour, bless us,	48
Dear Saviour, if these lambs should stray,	280
Depth of mercy,	129
Do not I love thee, O my Lord,	280
Earth has nothing sweet or fair,	154
Fading away like the dew,	17
Father, I stretch my hands,	126
Father, whate'er of earthly bliss,	280
Far, far away,	258
Fierce raged the tempest,	133
Forth to the land of promise,	33
Forward be our watchword,	36
For ever with the Lord,	286

INDEX OF FIRST LINES.

	PAGE
Friend of sinners,	7
From Greenland's icy mountains,	281
From every stormy wind that blows,	280
Galilean king and prophet,	267
Gently Lord, O gently lead us,	280
Glory be to God on high,	253
Glory be to God the Father,	211
Glorious things of thee are spoken,	112
God is love; his mercy brightens,	82
God is love, ye nations, hear him,	212
God's free mercy,	47
God moves in a mysterious way,	150
Go to dark Gethsemane,	194
Great God, at thy command,	237
Great God, we sing,	100
Guide me, O thou great Jehovah,	280
Hark, hark, my soul,	214
Hark, ten thousand harps and voices,	281
Hark, the sound of holy voices,	144
Hark, the air is full of voices,	88
Hark, hark, hear the blest tidings,	76
Hallelujah, praise the Lord,	6
Hallelujah,	84
Hear thy children,	204
Heavenly home,	96
He is coming,	66
He is gone,	136
Help us to praise thy name,	231
High in yonder realms,	242
Hitherto the Lord hath helped us,	32
How calm and beautiful the morn,	281
How firm a foundation,	282
How sweet the name of Jesus sounds,	282
Hold, thou, my hand,	25
Holy, holy, holy,	34
Hosanna, we sing,	200
Hosanna be the children's song,	94
Hosanna, Hosanna, Hosanna,	119
How can we sing,	209
How vain is all,	222
I am trusting thee,	49

	PAGE
I am not worthy,	123
I could not do without thee,	127
I bring my sins to thee,	207
I gave my life for thee,	59
I hear a sweet voice,	246
I have no help but thine,	74
I know that my Redeemer lives,	133
I lay my sins on Jesus,	256
I love the Sunday-school,	75
I love the sacred book,	237
I heard the voice of Jesus say,	282
I think I see it in the clouds,	106
I was a wandering sheep,	35
I want to do right,	210
I would be ready,	183
I will sing of that home,	188
I'm a pilgrim, and I'm a stranger,	283
I'm but a stranger here,	20
In the Christian's home in glory,	283
In his own raiment clad,	197
In the cross of Christ,	210
In thy name, O Lord,	140
In the hour of trial,	130
It came upon the midnight,	72
I've found the pearl,	91
Jesus, Jesus,	238
Jesus is our Shepherd,	193
Jesus, Master,	190
Jesus, I my cross have taken,	283
Jesus, meek and gentle,	53
Jesus, thou art the sinner's friend,	201
Jesus, thou hast bought us,	151
Jesus, whom angel hosts adore,	166
Jesus, in thy dying woes,	131
Jesus, my Saviour,	271
Jesus, Lord of life,	252
Jesus, we are far away,	196
Jesus is our Shepherd,	193
Jesus, lover of my soul,	174
Jesus, the very thought,	179
Jesus, still lead on,	40
Jesus, keep me near the cross,	274
Jerusalem, the golden,	186

INDEX OF FIRST LINES.

	PAGE.
Jerusalem, my happy home,	283
Journeying onward,	101
Just as I am,	177
Just as thou art,	182
Keep me near to thee,	14
Lamb of God,	137
Let all arise,	44
Let me come,	105
Let us go,	181
Lead, kindly light,	77
Light after darkness,	4
Light of the world,	146
Linger not,	224
Little raindrops,	100
List, list, list,	98
Lord, I hear,	178
Lord, I will follow thee,	184
Lord of mercy,	219
Lord God, the Holy Ghost,	251
Lord Jesus, by thy passion,	263
Lord, with glowing heart,	266
Lord, I care not for riches,	276
Lord Jesus, are we one,	143
Lord of earth,	18
Long from thee,	157
Maker of the Sabbath day,	262
Majestic sweetness sits enthroned,	284
Mary to the Saviour's tomb,	284
Meek and lowly,	264
More love to thee,	10
My days are gliding swiftly by,	178
My God, my Father,	90
My Saviour, as thou wilt,	30
Must Jesus bear the cross alone,	284
Nearer, my God, to thee,	20
Near the cross,	244
Not far from the kingdom,	158
Nothing either great or small,	180
Now I have found a Friend,	51
Now I have found the ground,	203

	PAGE.
O brother, be faithful,	60
O be joyful,	23
O bread, to pilgrims given,	12
O for a closer walk,	262
O gracious Lord,	223
O for a heart,	163
O Lord, how good,	191
Oh! how happy are they,	126
O eyes that are weary,	69
O happy saints,	87
O Lord of heaven,	194
O silent lamb,	243
O sweetly breathe,	228
O thou, heir of heaven,	261
O Rock of Ages,	154
O Saviour, precious Saviour,	156
O thou, the contrite sinner's friend,	270
O, where is he,	250
Of the Father's love,	135
Oh! were I bound,	249
Oh! for the robes,	247
One sweetly, solemn thought,	190
Of Jesus and his cross,	208
One there is,	108
Onward, Christian soldiers,	28
Once more, my soul,	245
Our blest Redeemer,	146
Palms of glory,	232
Pass me not,	259
Pilgrim, burdened,	52
Praise God, from whom,	163
Purer yet, and purer,	241
Return, O wanderer,	225
Rock of Ages,	172
Saviour, again,	19, 83
Saviour, I follow on,	107
Saviour, Lord,	199
See, oh! see,	229
See the conqueror,	255
Shout the tidings,	114, 235
Shall we meet,	56

INDEX OF FIRST LINES.

	PAGE.
Sing of Jesus,	103
Sing, my tongue,	150
Sing with all the sons,	115
Son of my soul, thou Saviour dear,	284
Soon will set,	218
Soon may the last glad song,	153
Softly and tenderly,	64
Soldiers of the cross,	26
Something, my God, for thee,	58
Sometimes a light surprises,	27, 192
Sowing in the morning,	55
Standing at the portal,	142
Stand up, stand up for Jesus,	260
Still will we trust,	138
Sweet as a shepherd's,	227
Sweetly sing the love,	16
Sweet hour of prayer,	171
Sweet the moments, rich in blessing,	284
Take up thy cross,	149
Take thy staff,	65
Take the world,	54
Take my heart,	153
Take my life,	11
Take the name of Jesus,	275
Ten thousand times,	50
The Homeland,	9
The day of resurrection,	254
The gospel ship,	185
The Saviour calls,	230
The Lord is my Shepherd,	69
The roseate hues,	145
There came three kings,	71
There is a green hill,	111
There is a land,	109
There is a book,	176
There is no little child,	173
There is a name,	240
There is a fountain filled with blood,	285
There is a happy land,	285
There is an hour of peaceful rest,	286
There's a beautiful home,	29
There's a friend,	202
There's a home,	102

	PAGE.
They who seek,	155
There's nothing sweeter,	86
There's a home for little children,	102
Thine for ever,	138
This is not my place,	160
This was a royal gift,	128
This is the day,	206
This morning, Lord,	195
Thou art coming,	132
Thou from whom,	68
Thou, whose almighty word,	189
Thou guardian,	223
Thou to whom,	134
To the place of graves,	37
To the wandering,	218
To thee, my God,	215
To thee, O Lord,	79
To our Redeemer's,	257
To the wandering and weary,	78
To-day the Saviour calls,	67
Toiling early,	21
To-morrow, Lord, is thine,	285
Through the night,	46
Thy way, not mine,	159
Through the love,	269
Till he come,	92
'Twas a watching group,	66
Thus far the Lord has led me on,	285
Upward where the stars,	148
Was there ever kindest Shepherd,	272
We are bound,	152
We are soldiers,	15
We are going,	226
We are travellers,	81
We march,	43
We're marching,	113
We're wandering,	124
Weary the way,	108
We have no refuge,	90
We need a Friend,	4
We praise thee, Heavenly Father,	112
We praise thee,	125

INDEX OF FIRST LINES.

	PAGE.		PAGE.
We praise thee with songs,	166	While we journey homeward,	22
We praise thee, O God,	125	Why have we lips,	110
Welcome, sweet day of rest,	281	With joy we hail,	82
What a Friend,	3	With such a groveling heart,	186
What happy children,	206	With tearful eyes,	164
What is it to believe,	183		
What is life?	233	Ye wretched, hungry,	13
When friend from friend,	230	Yes, for me,	8
When God of old,	251	Yet there is room,	57
When I survey,	198	Yield thy heart,	139
When shall we all meet,	41	Young children once,	221
When the sad hour,	187		

www.ingramcontent.com/pod-product-compliance
Lightning Source LLC
Chambersburg PA
CBHW032059220426
43664CB00008B/1068